THE UNRELUCTANT YEARS

The eager hours and unreluctant years

As on a dawn-illumined mountain stood . . .

Shelley, *Ode to Liberty*

THE UNRELUCTANT YEARS

A critical approach

to children's literature, by LILLIAN H. SMITH

American Library Association

Chicago, 1953

PERMISSION to quote the chapter mottoes has been given by the copyright owners:

Frances Clarke Sayers, *The Library Quarterly*, Vol. XIV, p.351-52, for chapter one,

George Sampson, *The Cambridge Book of Prose and Verse* (London: Cambridge Univ. Pr., 1942), p.xxxviii, for chapter two,

Anne Carroll Moore, *My Roads to Childhood* (N.Y.: Doubleday, 1939), p.24; and Geoffrey Trease, *Tales out of School* (London: Heinemann, 1948), p.11, for chapter three,

Annis Duff, *Bequest of Wings* (N.Y.: Viking, 1944), p.174, for chapter four,

Dorothy Hosford, *Thunder of the Gods* (N.Y.: Holt, 1952), p.107-110, for chapter five,

Walter de la Mare, *Come Hither* (N.Y.: Knopf, 1928), p.xxxiii, for chapter seven,

Anne Carroll Moore, *The Three Owls* (N.Y.: Macmillan, 1925), p.70, for chapter eight,

A. A. Milne, *Books for Children*, compiled by the National Book League (London: Cambridge Univ. Pr., 1948), p.4, for chapter nine,

H. Butterfield, *The Historical Novel* (London: Cambridge Univ. Pr., 1924), p.95-96, for chapter eleven,

Paul Hazard, *Books, Children and Men* (Boston: Horn Book, 1944), p.58, for chapter twelve.

TO THE CHILDREN'S LIBRARIANS
OF THE TORONTO PUBLIC LIBRARIES

FOREWORD

It is not the intention that this book should be an exhaustive guide to book selection for children, but rather that it should indicate the signposts which point the way toward a recognition of those qualities which are basic in good writing, whether in the books already familiar or in books yet to be published.

The following pages, therefore, contain no lists of suitable books for children. The aim of this book is to consider children's books as literature, and to discover some of the standards by which they can be so judged.

Children's books do not exist in a vacuum, unrelated to literature as a whole. They are a portion of universal literature and must be subjected to the same standards of criticism as any other form of literature. This basic principle should underlie all good book selection whatever kind of literature is being judged. So, in evaluating books for children, conviction that this is a literature of value and significance is an essential approach. Such conviction is gained only from sound knowledge of the material and critical analysis of each book in relation to the fundamental principles of good writing as found in literary classics.

A children's library of books, whether chosen for the home, the school or the public library, which has forgotten the rich inheritance of children's literature—its "classics"—betrays the special privilege of all such libraries and becomes only a means of further distributing mediocrity.

There are many forces in our life today which tend to separate the child and the book. Yet does not this make it only more desirable and more necessary that the best efforts be made to bring them together? If we must do things today for social causes, cannot a similar plea be made for good books for children? Was there ever a world or a time in which quality—the recognition and appreciation of quality—was more desperately needed?

The importance of the selective function in finding and making known the best in children's literature is the theme of this book. To tolerate the mediocre and the commonplace is to misunderstand the purpose of book selection and the significance of literature.

The variety and abundance of children's literature prevent any comprehensive discussion of every book of tested value. The books which have been chosen for analysis are a personal choice from the many books of permanent quality, and there is no suggestion that the books chosen are the only ones which repay appreciative study and analysis. Personal response to particular books is an individual matter and lends the urgency of conviction when books are discussed as literature rather than as commodities or tools. Children's literature is not a pedantic or an academic study. It is a joyous, fruitful and endlessly rewarding field.

While writing this book I have received constant consideration and encouragement from my Chief, Dr. Charles R. Sanderson. I have had the inspiration and help of the staff of the Toronto *Boys and Girls Division* and the invaluable aid of Frances Gray, my secretary. To M. Ethel Bubb of the Washington Public Library and to Charles C. Stotler of the Washington National Gallery I am indebted for their help with the chapter on Picture Books, which I acknowledge with grateful thanks.

Lillian H. Smith

CONTENTS

For [Paul Hazard] the realm of children's books is no small area of human accomplishment and knowledge, relegated to the teacher, the parent, and the librarian. He saw literature for children in relation to the driving, universal force of creative writing, wherever it appears in the world, whether it be addressed to children or adults. He acclaims those books which "remain faithful to the very essence of Art."

Frances Clarke Sayers,
"Books, Children and Men"
in *The Library Quarterly*

THE CASE FOR CHILDREN'S LITERATURE

 Within the pages of the *New England Primer* of the eighteenth century there is a crude woodcut of a child reading. Opposite the small picture is the couplet so often quoted,

> My book and heart
> Shall never part.

This attribute of childhood, this readiness of children to take to their hearts the books of their choice, while others apparently worthy lie neglected, has perplexed writers and publishers, booksellers and book buyers ever since John Newbery brought out his *Little Pretty Pocket Book* for the young masters and misses of his day.

No formula will solve the uncertainty, the perplexity of adults as to what children are looking for in the books they read. It cannot be confidently asserted that "children like this kind of book" or "children do not like that kind." Yet there is light to be had if we know where and how to look for it. When a new children's book is heralded as another *Alice in Wonderland* or another *Treasure Island* or *Tom Sawyer*, is it not an acknowledgment that these are books in which children have found what they are looking for? Does it not mean that a new book's claim to stand beside a well-loved favorite rests on the degree to which it possesses the magic of a Lewis Carroll or a Stevenson or a Mark Twain?

For there *is* magic in the writing of these books; a magic that enchants the children who read them as the tune of the Pied Piper lured the children of old Hamelin. It is a magic that eludes definition. The essence from which it is distilled can best be discovered in those books which generations of children have taken to their hearts and have kept alive, books which seem to have an immortality that adult books, so soon superseded by the latest best-seller, seldom attain.

12

The case for children's literature

Though we may not always know which individual book a child will take to his heart, there is less uncertainty as to *why* children read. Children are as aware of the pleasures of print, once they have discovered books, as any other part of the reading public. The children, like their elders, have found in books a kind of experience not to be gained in any other way. In a little book *Of Reading Books* by John Livingstone Lowes, we find Montaigne quoted, "I doe nothing without blithenesse," because, Lowes says, "that eager childlike zest once caught is seldom lost. There is no essential difference, for example, between Coleridge's absorption in *The Arabian Nights* and the irrepressible gusto with which John Keats read Shakespeare."[1] A child's experience of life is, necessarily, confined within the narrow limits of his environment. What he is looking for is a swift passage beyond its boundaries. Once he discovers this passage in a book, a child's instant transition seems to adults a gift of wings, whereas it is a simple and joyful willingness to go beyond those boundaries which are to him, for the time being, invisible.

No force in the world can compel children to read, for long, what they do not want. They defend their freedom of choice with great skill and persistence. They may not know why they reject one book and cling to another, for their judgment is seldom analytical. It is based on something genuine—pleasure—and "without blithenesse" they read reluctantly if at all.

A child's range of choice in his reading will always depend upon what is at hand, and this will largely depend upon his elders. Mistaken ideas among adults about what books a child likes, or should like, must prevent the very object they intend: a love for books and reading. If such misunderstanding is given widespread credence it will eventually affect what books are made generally available to children.

In an age of science, we have grown scientific about our children. They, as well, are reduced to formulas. We think of them in terms of I. Q.'s, of vocabulary range, of remedial reading. We present to them with great solemnity, but in words of one syllable, an explanation of the world about them exactly tailored to their capacities as we think we know them.

But what of the eager, reaching, elusive spirit of childhood which has its own far horizons, and a friendly and familiar acquaintance with miracle? Perhaps because of our modern tendency to believe in scien-

[1] John Livingstone Lowes, *Of Reading Books* (London: Constable, 1930), p.133.

tific methods we have forgotten to trust to certain inner capacities in children that lend themselves to no graph of age or progress, simply because we ourselves have left those capacities, that eagerness of vision, far behind and have long since forgotten them.

In his introduction to *Reading I've Liked* Clifton Fadiman tells of going over a manuscript for children written by Hendrik Van Loon and pointing out to him some long, difficult words which he thought children would not understand. Hendrik Van Loon's answer was merely "I put them in on purpose," and Clifton Fadiman comments "I learned later what he meant." A *good* writer for children has something to say; he says it in the best way possible and trusts the children to understand, as any study of the vocabulary of such writers as Lewis Carroll or Kenneth Grahame shows.

Walter de la Mare puts it this way:

> I know well that only the rarest kind of best in anything can be good enough for the young. I know too that in later life it is just (if only just) possible now and again to recover fleetingly the intense delight, the untellable joy and happiness and fear and grief and pain of our early years, of an all-but-forgotten childhood. I have, in a flash, in a momentary glimpse, seen again a horse, an oak, a daisy just as I saw them in those early years, as if with that heart, with those senses. It was a revelation.[2]

If we thought of children in that way, we should instinctively reject the mediocre, the unrewarding. We should put into their hands only the books worthy of them, the books of honesty, integrity, and vision—the books on which they can grow. For it is in the very nature of children to grow. They cannot stand still. They must have change and activity of both mind and body. Reading which does not stir their imaginations, which does not stretch their minds, not only wastes their time but will not hold children permanently. If they find no satisfaction in one medium they will immediately turn to another.

It is this sure instinct of children toward growth which ensures that what is permanent and of positive value in their reading will remain. For children, of all people, may be trusted to hold to that which seems to them good, since only in books having permanent values can they find the materials necessary for growth.

The thing that makes a book a good book to a child is that it is an experience. The child who has read and enjoyed such a book has grown

[2] Walter de la Mare, *Bells and Grass* (N.Y.: Viking, 1942), p.11.

14

a little, has added something to his stature as an individual. He is a little more capable of enjoying new impressions and receiving new ideas, which will illuminate his next new experience whatever it may be. He has gained something permanent which can never be taken away from him.

It is true that children go through stages in their reading as in their physical growth. A child may turn from reading fairy tales to books about the Vikings, or still later to an interest in Mars. But he will never lose the imaginative growth he gained from the fairy tales. His reading about the Vikings will leave with him a sense of history, of the long road man has traveled through ages past to the present. He will carry with him, too, the wonder of the universe gained from his own wonder and surmise about other worlds than ours. All that he reads "with blithenesse" will make a basis and a background for his further reading and will stimulate in him a desire, an actual necessity, to read more.

There is small danger that today's children will be any more willing to relinquish their literary heritage than the children of any other day, so long as their own "great books" are put within their reach. "All spirit" wrote Thomas Traherne, "is mutually attractive." The spirit of childhood in each generation is attracted to the spirit of the writers of those books who collectively have given them a children's literature.

But let us make sure that we are all thinking of the same thing when we are thinking of children's literature. All books written for children are not necessarily literature, nor does the adult's conception of what constitutes a children's book coincide always with that of the child. There are those who think of a child's book as just a simpler treatment of an adult theme. This point of view considers children only as diminutive adults and arises from a misunderstanding of childhood itself. For children are a race whose experience of life is different from that of adults. Theirs is a different world—a child's world in which values are expressed in children's terms and not in those which belong to adult experience.

For instance, children's problems are simpler than those of their elders, yet, at the same time, cut nearer to the heart of things than those of adults. Children perceive the abstract distinction between the true and the false, the good and the bad, happiness and sorrow, justice and injustice, rather than the particular applications of these principles which cause their elders so much concern. Good children's books are clear cut in their issues. Their values are sound and directly put. Yet they do not preach these principles, rather are they implicit in the writing. In their reading of fairy tales, for example, children are persuaded that "unselfish and faithful love always ends by finding its reward, *be it only in oneself*" (mark you!) and they discover "how ugly and low are envy, jealousy and greed." And these are some of the things that children want to know.

Children may not consciously recognize their search for lasting truth in their indiscriminate reading of fairy tales, high adventure, humorous stories, and all the variety of literature that brings delight and rouses a warm response in their minds. But they are aware of the implications beneath the surface in their reading, that here are truths they can hold to. A sense of security comes not only from a provision of material needs. It must have its roots within the individual. It should cause small wonder if, without these roots, children lack stability and reflect only the confused values with which our contemporary life is surrounded. Good children's books give those who enjoy them a steadying power, like a sheet anchor in a high wind, not moral at all, but something to hold to.

Another misconception with regard to children's reading must be mentioned here. Because we are adults so long and childhood is so brief and fleeting, it is assumed that the experience of childhood is relatively so much the less important. Yet childhood is the impressionable and formative period, so receptive and so brief that a child has less need of and less time for the mediocre than an adult. The impressions of childhood are lasting, and the sum of its impressions is the pattern taken on by maturity. If this be true, the child is indeed father to the man. Can we then afford to be indifferent to the impressions that children receive from their reading?

There are those who regard children only as potential adult readers and think it does not matter greatly what they read as children. We do indeed hope that children will continue to read after they become adults, yet would anyone doubt that a child who, for instance, has read *Treasure Island,* has had an immediate experience which lights a child's world where he is? The impact of even one good book on a child's mind is surely an end in itself, a valid experience which helps him to form standards of judgment and taste at the time when his mind is most sensitive to impressions of every kind. The reading in childhood of *Treasure Island,* or any good book, may well be a prelude to further reading carried into adult life. The strong and lasting impression of such a prelude will bring to adult reading some recognition of vitality and permanence.

Still another misconception of adults is the tendency to think that children's books exist in a vacuum, unrelated to literature as a whole. Yet it becomes evident from attentive and considered reading of children's literature that identical artistic standards prevail in both children's and adult literature. The fact that there is a body of children's literature standing squarely on its own merit should persuade anyone interested in literature to regard it seriously. And those adults who give, or intend to give, their time and energy, their capacity and ability to the appraisal of children's books should have a conviction that children's literature as *literature* is significant, with its values rooted in the tradition of all literature. C. S. Lewis says this differently when he tells us that "no book is really worth reading at the age of ten which is not equally (and often far more) worth reading at the age of fifty . . . the only imaginative works we ought to grow out of are those which it would have been better not to have read at all."[3]

There is a key that will open (or reopen) to adults the door of the imaginative world of children's books. It is the same key that the children hold—pleasure—although it may be a different kind of pleasure from a child's, since an adult brings to his reading of a children's book his whole experience of life, his association of ideas, and his mature taste and discrimination. For instance, one kind of enjoyment which adults find in children's books as literature is an enjoyment of which children are seldom consciously aware; a pleasure in the order and beauty of words, in the art of writing, that is similar to listening to music or looking at a picture. When Kenneth Grahame in *The Wind in the Willows* set the stage for the Piper at the Gates of Dawn, he chose for the setting the familiar and friendly river on which Mole and Rat are slowly paddling upstream waiting for the moon. Here is the picture of the scene Kenneth Grahame paints in words:

> The line of the horizon was clear and hard against the sky, and in one particular quarter it showed black against a silvery climbing phosphorescence that grew and grew. At last, over the rim of the waiting earth the moon lifted with slow majesty till it swung clear of the horizon and rode off, free of moorings, and once more they

[3] C. S. Lewis, "On Stories," in *Essays Presented to Charles Williams* (London: Oxford, 1947), p.100.

> began to see surfaces—meadows widespread, and quiet gardens, and the river itself from bank to bank, all softly disclosed, all washed clean of mystery and terror, all radiant again as by day, but with a difference that was tremendous. Their old haunts greeted them again in other raiment, as if they had slipped away and put on this pure new apparel and come quietly back, smiling as they shyly waited to see if they would be recognized again under it.[4]

Children will not savor the quality of such description for its own sake, yet even they feel an element of mystery which adds to their absorption in the story of Otter's rescue, so dramatically told in this chapter.

Children's literature is so complex a subject that a consideration of its every aspect is too lengthy and involved to be attempted in a single book. Nor is it possible to examine every individual book of value. Our aim is to weigh as literature certain children's books, which represent various kinds of children's reading interests, and to indicate some of the standards by which they can be judged. The tradition of children's literature will be briefly considered, not as a history of quaint and bygone relics, but to show the growth of literature for children through the books that have lived to the present day.

There are principles of criticism which are applicable to literature in general. These we will consider with regard to their application in judging the merit of children's books. In the various fields of writing for children we will discuss and analyze the qualities of certain established children's "classics" in these fields, which will help us to form sound judgments of newer books as they appear. Children read for information, as well as for imaginative delight, and although "books of knowledge" are only incidentally literature, we will discuss briefly their requirements in their own special fields. A short list of associative reading will follow each chapter.

Writing for children is an art and should be approached as such. In this discussion of children's books the emphasis will be on books as literature, as an end in themselves, and not as tools serving a secondary purpose, however worthy. To regard children's books in this way, to ask that they make to a child's growth, intellectual and spiritual, a contribution of permanent value, is not to lay an undue weight upon a subject that should be a lighthearted and happy one.

[4] Kenneth Grahame, *The Wind in the Willows* (N.Y.: Scribner, 1933), p.157.

The case for children's literature

Whatever form a children's book may take, whether a fairy tale, a fantasy, or a book of heroic adventure, let us approach it with an open mind and heart for its power to move us by the beauty and truth it may hold within its covers. Ever since the days of Oliver Goldsmith and Charles Lamb great writers have given children's literature a growing and widening importance. Surely there can be no condescension in our approach to the books for children by writers such as John Ruskin, Charles Kingsley, Nathaniel Hawthorne, Lewis Carroll, George Macdonald, W. H. Hudson, Mark Twain, Howard Pyle, John Masefield, R. L. Stevenson, and others, whose books have long been acknowledged as literature of distinction. Modern writers of considerable reputation in the field of general literature are writing children's books whose creative quality is unquestioned. On all these books, and on those of other creative writers who choose solely the field of children's books for writing, we rest the case for children's literature.

ASSOCIATIVE READING

DUFF, ANNIS. "Bequest of Wings"; a Family's Pleasures with Books. Viking, 1944.

EATON, ANNE THAXTER. Reading with Children. Viking, 1940.

EYRE, FRANK. Twentieth Century Children's Books. Longman's, Green, 1952.

HAZARD, PAUL. Books, Children and Men; tr. from the French by Margaret Mitchell. Horn Book, 1944.

The Horn Book Magazine. vol. 1– October, 1924– .

MOORE, ANNE CARROLL. My Roads to Childhood; Views and Reviews of Children's Books. Doubleday, Doran, 1939.

REPPLIER, AGNES. What Children Read (in Books and Men). Houghton, Mifflin, 1888.

WHITE, DOROTHY NEAL. About Books for Children. Oxford Univ. Pr., 1947.

CHAPTER TWO

As we read our older literature charitably, let us also read it wisely, discriminating frankly between what is good and what is only quaint or curious. Great literature survives by its intrinsic and absolute worth. It is right to admire a poem for its absolute value; it is right to admire a poem for its historical value; but it is wrong to mistake one value for the other.

George Sampson,
The Cambridge Book of Prose and Verse

THE LINEAGE OF CHILDREN'S LITERATURE

As far in the past as we have any record, the stories that were told around the hearth, the folk tales, the tales that were sung by wandering minstrels in the great halls, were the universal oral literature of all, young and old. When the printed word replaced the storyteller and the minstrel, when learning and literature emerged from the mists of time, the stories and ballads still lived on in the minds and hearts of the unlettered and simple folk. Wanda Gag has summed up the process in her introduction to *Gone Is Gone*. "This," she says, "is an old, old story. When I was a little girl my grandmother told it to me. When she was a little girl she heard it from her grandfather and when he was a little boy in Bohemia his mother told it to him. Where she heard it from I do not know, but you can see it is an old, old story."[1]

This common traditional literature, shared alike by adults and children, was not overlooked when the printed book brought literature within the reach of all who could read. Caxton, the first English printer, chose to print *Reynard the Fox* (1481) and *The Fables of Aesop* (1484) among the earliest books on his list. Caxton was a practical businessman and he printed what he knew the public would buy, the well-loved tales familiar in oral tradition. In fact, the combined efforts of Caxton and de Worde, his successor, inadvertently provided an excellent children's library which included *The Fables of Aesop, Reynard the Fox*, the stories of *Guy of Warwick, Bevis of Hampton, Valentine and Orson, Robin Hood, Havelok the Dane* and *King Arthur*. All of these are among the tales we now consider basic children's stories.

[1]Copyright, 1935, by Wanda Gag. Reprinted by permission of Coward-McCann, Inc.

21

The unreluctant years

A common knowledge of this oral tradition was taken for granted by writers before books became plentiful and cheap. Shakespeare quoted from *Mr. Fox* when he wrote *Much Ado about Nothing* and from *Childe Rowland* in *King Lear,* although at that time the stories were still unprinted—and children today, who read Jacobs' *English Fairy Tales,* can be heard chanting "Be bold, be bold, but not too bold," and the dark tower of Childe Rowland is to them still a place of mystery and magic.

It would be an interesting study to follow the history of the printing and reprinting of all these tales, but in a brief account of the books which have given children's literature its place in all literature it is possible to note only the first appearance of those books which have become fixed stars in literature for children. These fixed stars were not written with children in mind, but without exception they are books which children have made their own, in which they continue to find delight, and consequently are a guide to what pleases children.

It is true that while children often accept what is offered to them, they also reach for what they want, though they may not understand the imaginative and dramatic instinct that makes them want it. This gift of wonder, of longing, of reaching out—call it what you will—belongs to children as it belonged to the childhood of the race. The years of childhood, before self-consciousness in any acute way comes over them, are the years of wonder, the years when a child will find and exploit all that his active and ranging mind can lay hold of. In books, and perhaps in nothing else so much as books, can he find such richness of opportunity. This natural instinct of a child toward beauty and imagination explains why the picture of children's literature must be a composite one; why it is made up of what the children have taken for themselves, as well as what they have been given.

Children reached out for the Puritan masterpiece, *Pilgrim's Progress,* when it appeared in 1678. They recognized in it a fairy tale with adventures not unlike those of Jack the Giant-Killer, and as marvellous. They even made a game of it, and taking sticks and hats, with bundles on their backs, they started off on an imaginary journey, getting past the lions, fighting the foul fiend Apollyon, being imprisoned in Doubting Castle, wandering upon the Delectable Mountains, and at last entering the shining gate of the King's Palace.

Perhaps John Bunyan was aware of the children's interest in the book he had written and was encouraged to write a book he called

Divine Emblems intended directly for boys and girls. But the children would have none of it. They did not care for his rhymed moralizings on birds and insects. They recognized a *purpose* and fought shy. True, *Pilgrim's Progress* had a purpose too, but the drama of the story rose triumphant over all, while *Divine Emblems* crumbled into dust, and dust it has remained.

Then, when the Puritan influence was growing fainter, but before the kindling of interest in the child and his reading in the eighteenth century, two more books, intended for their elders, were taken over by the children: *Robinson Crusoe* (1719) and *Gulliver's Travels* (1726). As Paul Hazard has said in *Books, Children and Men*:

> What is there so surprising in their seizing upon *Robinson Crusoe*, if they find it to be a story of constructive ingenuity and energy? They also start out in life rather fearful. Like their great ship-wrecked friend, they find themselves tossed onto an unknown land whose limits they will never know except by slow exploration. Like him, they are afraid of the darkness that falls. Night arrives and closes them in. Who knows if the sun will appear again tomorrow? They have everything to fear, beginning with hunger, with cold. Little by little they gain poise, are reassured, and begin to live on their own account. Just as Robinson does when he starts out to re-construct his life.[2]

Dean Swift never intended his stinging, biting satire, *Gulliver's Travels*, for children. It is interesting to speculate what he would have said, had someone told him that the book he worked at so savagely, night after night, in his big lonely house in Ireland, would be the delight of many generations of boys and girls. There is much in *Gulliver's Travels* that children cannot understand. They take what they like from it; and what they like best is the inexhaustible imagination that pictured and peopled the Lilliputian world in which Gulliver has such entertaining adventures, and the equally surprising and laughable predicaments of Gulliver in Brobdingnag among the giants. To them it is a story, as alive today as when it first appeared in 1726.

Across the Channel in France, meantime, Charles Perrault had written his version of eight fairy tales of France, published in 1698 under the title of *Histoires ou Contes du temps passé*. Perrault's fairy tales were translated into English and appeared in print not long

[2] Paul Hazard, *Books, Children and Men* (Boston: Horn Book, 1944), p.58.

after *Gulliver's Travels* was first published. Although a few folk tales had been printed separately in the crude form of chap books, Perrault's was the first collection of fairy tales to appear in English. It contained "The Sleeping Beauty," "Red Riding Hood," "Blue Beard," "Puss-in-Boots," "Diamonds and Toads," "Cinderella," "Riquet with the Tuft," and "Hop-o'-my-Thumb"; stories which have become the universal and immortal possession of children of every generation.

All this took place before John Newbery hung out his shingle as a bookseller in St. Paul's Churchyard at the sign of the Bible and Sun. His shingle was also a sign that a consciously designed literature for children was on the way. John Newbery's was a lone voice at the time when he began printing little books especially for children. He seems to have been both aware of this potential market and astute enough to take advantage of it. John Newbery was a commercial genius. We see him at this time employing Smollett to edit a magazine, printing and selling innumerable little books for children, and keeping an eye on Oliver Goldsmith, who boarded near by, advancing small funds to him from time to time which Goldsmith repaid by his writings.

We have good reason to believe that Goldsmith was the author of *Goody Two Shoes,* the first book written directly for children in English which has survived. It has lived because it was written by an author who put the story and its characters before the moral purpose. True, *Goody Two Shoes* has a moral. Its writer had obviously a passion for justice and an intimate knowledge of the hard lot of the small farmer in the early part of the eighteenth century. But he could also tell a story in an intimate, confiding tone. In *Goody Two Shoes* he created a child, who, if she were real, would be one whom children would like. The little story has that nameless quality that has kept alive the interest of both adults and children through the years.

Goldsmith may also have been the unidentified collector of the nursery rhymes printed by Newbery's shop under the title of *Mother Goose's Melody.* The association of Mother Goose with these indestructible rhymes of the nursery is so inseparable to us today that it is hard to believe that this is the first record we have which connects the two. The origin of the rhymes remains forever in the field of conjecture. For the most part they are as old as the hills and in their continuity and familiarity are as much a part of the tradition of childhood as "Cinderella," "The Sleeping Beauty," and "The Three Little Pigs."

24

The lineage of children's literature

Mother Goose's Melody contained over fifty of the rhymes and, surprisingly, included at the end some of the lyric songs from Shakespeare's plays. A much enlarged collection of nursery rhymes was made by Halliwell and published in 1849 as *Popular Rhymes and Nursery Tales,* a collection which has been the source of many of the modern editions of Mother Goose for children.

Although nursery rhymes and ballads were familiar to children of this period there had so far been little else in verse form which they had spontaneously taken for their own. Then *Songs of Innocence* appeared in 1788 and the music of their pure poetry has been sounding in children's ears to the present day. Blake chose his title well. These poems are innocent of any subterfuge, innocent of literary devices. They flow directly and naturally from the heart of a great poet. Their keynote is simplicity. They are like the nursery rhymes in their simplicity of form, their purity of diction, and the boldness and brevity of the pictures they create. Perhaps that is why children have recognized as their own the poetry of one of the great names in English literature.

The books written for children after *Goody Two Shoes* and until the close of the eighteenth century, the "Age of Reason" as it has been called, were the natural outcome of a period that shut the door on imagination. None of these strongly didactic books for children have survived except as curiosities, since their authors ignored the nature, the environment, and the inclination of the children for whom they wrote.

In a letter to Coleridge, Charles Lamb complains that

> *Goody Two Shoes* is almost out of print. Mrs. Barbauld's stuff has banished all the old classics of the nursery . . . Science has succeeded to poetry no less in the little walks of children than with men. Is there no possibility of averting this sore evil? Think what you would have been now, if instead of being fed with tales and old wives' fables in childhood, you had been crammed with geography and natural history!

Lamb did more than complain, however, for in 1806 Godwin published *Tales from Shakespeare,* told for children by Charles and Mary Lamb.

It must have been a happy surprise to a child of that day, as it still is to children today, to find his first introduction to Shakespeare not so difficult after all. For there is a freshness about these stories as if they were being told for the first time. Scenes from the plays are pictured with a clarity and precision that send one to the original play to see how so many details could have been missed in one's own reading.

The success of the *Tales* was immediate and a number of editions appeared during Lamb's lifetime. In the field of general literature in England it would be difficult to recall another title published at this time which today is as popular as the *Tales,* or even read at all. The Lambs did their work so well that no later attempt to make narratives of Shakespeare's plays has equalled their freshness. The *Tales from Shakespeare* stand on their own as literature.

The *Tales* were followed in 1808 by *The Adventures of Ulysses* retold for children by Charles Lamb from Chapman's translation, and not from the original Homer which Lamb had never read. Nevertheless as Mr. Harvey Darton says: "Lamb achieved the strange feat of getting some of the Odyssey's glorious ease with what might almost be simple Elizabethan prose."[3] There have been many children's retellings of Homer since then, but Charles Lamb's *Adventures of Ulysses* is a classic in its own right and his is still the most literary retelling of the story of Ulysses for children.

The work of the Lambs on behalf of children's literature revealed that the door to imagination was opening. There was also a growing interest among writers and scholars in preserving the genuine traditional tales still being told among the common folk. These they began to collect with laborious care, writing them down with scrupulous fidelity in the very words of the storyteller. Although the interest of the scholars was largely in the light these folk tales cast on ancient beliefs, customs, and superstitions, children found the stories packed with humor and drama, beauty, and wonder.

Folk tales, apart from Perrault's collection and a few stories printed separately such as *Tom Hickathrift, Jack the Giant Killer,* and *Jack and the Beanstalk,* were preserved only in oral literature. In Germany, however, two brothers, Jakob and Wilhelm Grimm, were taking down by word of mouth the folk tales told by the simple German peasants; and these stories were published in Germany as *Kindermärchen* in 1812-1824. Shortly after their appearance the tales were translated into English by Edgar Taylor with an introduction by John Ruskin

[3] F. J. Harvey Darton, *Children's Books in England* (N.Y.: Macmillan, 1932), p.199. This and the quotations on pages 27 and 28 are used by permission.

and with illustrations by George Cruikshank. The English title given to Grimm's collection, *Household Tales,* was prophetic, for there is probably no other children's book which has become so universally a household word as Grimm's fairy tales.

The immediate popularity of the folk tales collected by the Grimm brothers showed the way by which the imaginative needs of children could find the best kind of sustenance. But it was not until Mary Howitt translated Hans Andersen's fairy tales that children's literature was once more enriched by a work of genius, and again it was a gift from European sources. *Wonderful Stories for Children* by Hans Andersen, translated by Mary Howitt, was published in 1846. Since then, new translations have appeared at intervals; and the strong imagination and deep sensitiveness to the soul of things in Andersen's stories have made them inevitably an enduring heritage for children everywhere. As Harvey Darton says in *Children's Books in England,* Andersen's fairy tales "blended for the first time and for all time the strains of fantasy and folklore. Andersen's tales contain both elements in a pure state."

The Victorian interest in romantic literature was reflected in England in the books written for Victorian children. The winds of opinon about what children should read veered toward romance, laughter, and imagination. In the same year that Mary Howitt translated Andersen's fairy tales, Edward Lear published *The Book of Nonsense,* an inconsequent and hilarious collection of verses whose accented rhythms and humorous drawings have an irresistible charm.

The children of England and America have always shared a common heritage of literature. This is especially true of the great children's books, the pathfinders which have blazed new trails in the country of imagination, whether written in America or in England. In the Golden Age of children's literature, which flowered in the second half of the nineteenth century, Nathaniel Hawthorne retold twelve of the Greek legends. They were published in two volumes, *The Wonder Book* (1852), followed the next year by *Tanglewood Tales.* Hawthorne's retelling of these ancient stories is warm and intimate, closer to the fairy-tale tradition than Charles Kingsley's version which he called *The Heroes.* Kingsley's book, published in 1856, contained some of the same stories as *The Wonder Book* and *Tanglewood Tales.* Much of his writing is reminiscent of the beauty and dignity of Greek poetry.

The unreluctant years

Charles Kingsley's most famous book for children is, of course, *The Water-Babies,* which appeared in 1863. While written with a moral purpose, even a devout purpose, the story of little Tom is so imaginatively and sincerely told that the book still weaves a spell for little children.

The fantasy of *The Water-Babies* was a prelude to a greater fantasy, a work of sheer genius, which has become the timeless and ageless possession of childhood wherever it is read. *Alice in Wonderland* by Lewis Carroll was published in 1865 and has influenced the whole character and idea of writing for children ever since. The second Alice, *Through the Looking Glass,* no less a work of genius than the first book, was not published until 1871, six years after *Alice in Wonderland.* During that interval, in 1868, Louisa May Alcott in New England published *Little Women,* with characters drawn from New England life and scenes. Alice M. Jordan writes (in *From Rollo to Tom Sawyer):* "No other American story for girls has reached a wider circle, no other heroine has been so well loved as dear, honest, openhearted Jo March, best drawn because best known by Louisa Alcott."[4]

There are books that are contributions to children's literature for a generation, but which are so fitted into the social framework of their time that they afterwards lose much of their significance. The convention within which the characters of such a story as, for instance, Catherine Sinclair's *Holiday House* live, becomes a matter of social history. But when Mark Twain looked back on his own boyhood on the Mississippi, it was not only an era that he illuminated but the heart of universal and eternal boyhood. Five years after the appearance of Louisa Alcott's famous *Little Women, Tom Sawyer* was published, followed by *Huckleberry Finn* in 1885, and as Harvey Darton says, "They are attached to the Mississippi, but they are part of the world."

Meanwhile, in England, still another fantasy had appeared to take its place beside *The Water-Babies* and *Alice in Wonderland. At the Back of the North Wind* by George Macdonald has a pure imaginative quality whose essence of spiritual truth lingers in the mind of the sensitive reader, who has found the same quality in his earlier reading of fairy tales and in Andersen's stories.

So far, no book of breathless adventure for children was to be found in their literature. It must have been a fresh and exciting experience to the boys and girls of Robert Louis Stevenson's day when he wrote

[4] Alice M. Jordan, *From Rollo to Tom Sawyer* (Boston: Horn Book, 1948), p.38.

Treasure Island in 1882, with its theme of buried treasure, pirates, and mutiny at sea. The immense popularity of *Treasure Island* revealed the wide interest of children in this theme and opened the field for other books of romantic adventure, but Stevenson's Long John Silver has remained to this day the greatest pirate of them all. Still another new trail was blazed when Rudyard Kipling's *Jungle Book* appeared in 1894. All the color and mystery, the life and allure of the Indian jungle and its animal inhabitants, are found in these incomparable stories which tell how Mowgli, the boy, shared the precarious life of the wolf pack and its gathering on council rock.

The great variety of books written for children in this last half of the nineteenth century, extending also into the early part of the twentieth century, can only be indicated by the developments which were most marked and have influenced the trend of writing for children up to the present time. The most interesting developments were:

(1) The collecting and publishing of children's editions of folk and fairy tales such as Grimm's *Household Tales,* Dasent's *Popular Tales from the Norse,* Andersen's *Fairy Tales,* Joseph Jacob's *English Fairy Tales,* The Andrew Lang "colored" *Fairy Books* and Joel Chandler Harris' *Uncle Remus.*

(2) The retelling of Greek legends and of the epic stories such as Hawthorne's *Wonder Book* and *Tanglewood Tales,* Kingsley's *The Heroes,* Alfred Church's *Story of the Iliad* and *Story of the Odyssey,* Howard Pyle's *The Story of King Arthur and His Knights* and Sidney Lanier's *The Boy's King Arthur.*

(3) The advent of stories of pure imagination such as *Alice in Wonderland, The Water-Babies, At the Back of the North Wind, The King of the Golden River, The Rose and the Ring* and Stockton's *Fanciful Tales.*

(4) An interest in the sincere and revealing stories of everyday boyhood and girlhood such as *Little Women, Hans Brinker, Tom Sawyer* and *Stalky,* and the "family" stories of Mrs. Ewing, E. Nesbit and Lucretia Hale's *The Peterkins.*

(5) The interest in historical events and times, stimulated by the writings of Sir Walter Scott, found its way into such books for children as Charlotte Yonge's *The Little Duke* and *The Lances of Lynwood,* Mark Twain's *The Prince and the Pauper,* Conan Doyle's *Sir Nigel,* Howard Pyle's *Otto of the Silver Hand* and *Men of Iron,* and John Bennett's *Master Skylark* and *Barnaby Lee,* while for a purely romantic

and adventurous interest we note such books as *Treasure Island, Twenty Thousand Leagues Under the Sea* and *Jim Davis. The Jungle Book* seems to stand by itself; although its influence in opening up the field of animal life and character as a reading interest of children is unquestionable.

While the stature of these writers who wrote books for children before the twentieth century (or in its early years) has made its tradition one of great distinction and originality, the vitality of children's literature is shown in its steady growth to the present day. The great variety and volume of children's books published in this twentieth century can only be mentioned in the limits of so brief a survey. In any effort to evaluate their merit, the yardstick we use must be one we have gained through familiarity with the best that has been written in the past, for our trust will in the end rest upon the master-pieces of children's literature.

Growth is a sign of life. The writing of books for children is a living art and it should be approached as such, not as a static thing which has stood still since *Alice in Wonderland* appeared. Alice, and such books as *The Heroes* and *The Wind in the Willows,* may be our touch-stones by which we can judge the claims of newer books to stand beside these giants, though they may be giants in a Lilliputian world. But the fact remains that fine children's books continue to be published, and new children's classics are being written and are still to be written. Of this heritage of children's literature, the following chapters will try to present some composite critical understanding and analysis.

ASSOCIATIVE READING

BARRY, FLORENCE V. A Century of Children's Books. Doran, 1923. Methuen, 1922.

DARTON, F. J. HARVEY. Children's Books in England; Five Centuries of Social Life. Macmillan, 1932. Cambridge Univ. Pr., 1932.

FIELD, Mrs. E. M. The Child and His Book; Some Account of the History and Progress of Children's Literature in England. Wells Gardner, Darton, 1891.

FOLMSBEE, BEULAH. A Little History of The Horn-Book. Horn Book, 1942.

HEWINS, CAROLINE M. A Mid-Century Child and Her Books. Macmillan, 1926.

JAMES, PHILIP. Children's Books of Yesterday, ed. by C. Geoffrey Holme. Studio, 1933.

JORDAN, ALICE MABEL. From Rollo to Tom Sawyer, and Other Papers. Horn Book, 1948.

MEIGS, CORNELIA, and others. A Critical History of Children's Literature. Macmillan, 1953.

REPPLIER, AGNES. Little Pharisees in Fiction (in *Varia*). Houghton, Mifflin, 1897.

SMITH, ELVA S. The History of Children's Literature. American Library Assn., 1937.

TURNER, E. S. Boys Will Be Boys. Michael Joseph, 1948.

WELSH, CHARLES. A Bookseller of the Last Century. Griffith, Farran, Okeden and Welsh, 1885.

WHITE, GLEESON. Children's Books and Their Illustrators. Studio, 1897-98.

CHAPTER THREE

Not indiscriminate praise in the advertising of all of the children's books of a season, but informed criticism of good work and poor work is the need of our time. Without it we cannot hope for any considerable amount of distinctive, original writing in a field whose readers are its truest critics.

Anne Carroll Moore,
My Roads to Childhood

It is always warming to be liked, but the function of [critics] is not to warm me, or any other author. It is to tell us, through competent judges of style and content, whether we are writing well or badly.

Geoffrey Trease,
Tales out of School

AN APPROACH TO CRITICISM

Probably the first question that occurs to anyone who picks up a book is, "What is it about?" A casual reader can find a casual answer on the title page, or in the table of contents, or from the blurb on the book jacket. He can discover that it is a book about an arctic explorer, or about a boy who runs away to sea, or it may be about a pioneer family in the Middle West. Such a cursory glance may satisfy random curiosity and determine a book's immediate appeal, but the critical reader has more than a casual question to ask of the book he appraises.

The publisher's reader who reads the manuscript of a book, the critic who reviews it, the librarian who selects it for a children's library, may individually view the same book from differing points of view. The publisher's reader may consider it from the standpoint of its potential returns to the publishing house concerned. The critic in writing his review is concerned with bringing the book to the particular public for which it will hold interest. The librarian, on the other hand, will consider the book's suitability to take its place in a carefully selected collection. The final judgment, although arrived at from different points of view, should be based on similar principles; on a knowledge of literature and on a conception of literary standards, for on these the authority of any appraisal rests.

This is to say, a critic or book-selector must know what he expects to find in a book; and he must know what the standards are that must be met. He must be able to recognize those qualities which are basic in good writing whether in the books already familiar or in books newly published; whether in the field of general literature or in the special field we call children's literature.

Many factors help to produce numbers of children's books that are not literature. The publishing of children's books has become a profitable field as we see when we find it stands second only to fiction in the number of books of all classes of literature published in any year. When we consider the number of children's books arriving from the press the matter becomes fundamental. There is a real possibility that the fine book may pass unnoticed, or undistinguishable, even if included in an omnibus review, simply because serious attention to children's books is all but absent in contemporary criticism. There is good, bad, and indifferent writing to be found in every field. But what would become of our culture if the fine novel, poem, or play was a matter of indifference to us and was neglected in the critical press, merely because of lack of general interest in that particular form of literary achievement? And surely, the fine children's book in which literature is attained is as valid and as worthy of serious criticism as any other good book.

The short history of children's literature has shown that many of the worst features of an era are accented in the children's books of each period. We know how certain subjects of temporary concern can become so predominant as to influence what books are given to children, as for example the "good godly books" written for children of the Puritan era which were overloaded with precocious goodness, morbid piety, and sickly sentiment. Our own time, with its awakened concern for minority groups and sense of social injustice, has not been unwilling to burden children's books with what Anne Carroll Moore has called "lifeless stories with too much background and too many problems." Such books are too often applauded by adults because they reflect a grownup's sincere concern for social problems, rather than because the theme is a natural interest of childhood. Nor is the permanent literary value of these books given careful scrutiny.

In a world of unrest dominated by science and materialism, is it reasonable or wise to fail in setting up standards of values in the field of contemporary writing for children? The development and use of a personal yardstick gained from and based on the classics of children's literature, if applied to any newly published book, will help us to recognize those books which share, in varying degrees, the ingredients of the books which have shown enduring qualities. The need for such a yardstick is obvious, toward the end that among the great numbers of books being published, with the impetus of commercialism and materialism giving undue authority and prominence to the merely mediocre, we shall be able to recognize those qualities which are basic in good writing. Children have wide individual differ-

34

ences in taste and preference; but the recognition of an underlying soundness or unsoundness in writing, theme, and content will serve to keep in the field of children's books those that will bring a deeper and more lasting pleasure to children.

The qualities which are basic in good writing are literary values: that is, they do not concern the subject matter so much as how it is presented. The subject matter of a book may be eminently sensible, and the presentation of it pre-eminently dull. In other cases, the subject matter may be nonsense, yet the presentation of it suggests the most profound truths. What other inference can be drawn than that the subject makes less difference than the writer's presentation of it, so far as the book being or not being literature is concerned? "It is the art which gives the value and not the material." The success of *Robinson Crusoe*, for instance, revealed that the subject matter of shipwreck on a desert island was one of great interest to the reading public, especially to children. A host of imitators seized on the idea and stories of castaways appeared in great numbers. Most of these have fallen by the wayside and passed into oblivion, while *Robinson Crusoe*, after over two centuries, continues to be "the best desert island story ever written." Defoe created in *Robinson Crusoe* a fundamental and universal conception which his imitators never achieved.

A clear understanding of the fundamental principles of good writing should underlie all informed book criticism and selection, whatever kind of book is being judged. There is not one set of values for one class of book and another set for another group; there are certain basic principles which apply to all. They are best discovered by the critic or reviewer who asks such questions of a book as: What did the author intend to do? What means did he employ? Did he succeed? If his success was partial, where did he fail? That is to say, the reviewer's approach to the book he is reviewing will be an analytical one.

To analyze precisely is not the cold scientific dissection that it sounds. It is rather the first condition for understanding the difference between a good book and a poor one. The analysis of a book helps us to arrive at certain conclusions. But the validity of these conclusions depends on the qualities the reviewer brings to the book as well as on those of the book itself. To learn to evaluate and analyze is to learn to read with mind and heart, with interest and sympathy. To read this way brings excitement to the discovery of the idea of the writer behind the writing and of his use of language to express his idea. On the other hand, while one book may arouse enthusiasm, to another our response may be disappointment. In either case it will be wise to analyze the causes of each reaction.

The qualities a reviewer brings to a book are important. Enthusiasm that is uninformed is untrustworthy and adverse criticism based on prejudice is equally so. A sincere critic makes an effort to separate his personal opinions from his literary judgments and to have a reason for the faith that is in him. It is the *why* of criticism that is the test of our judgment of a book: why do we like it, or why do we not? When we know this, then only can we claim to have penetrated beneath the surface of a book. Otherwise our opinion is no more considered than that of any casual or superficial reader. "To like and dislike rightly," Bosanquet wrote, "is the goal of all culture worth the name." It is also the goal of the sincere critic of any form of literature.

Does this analytical approach spoil for us, when we use it, the freshness and spontaneity with which we come to a book? It need not, if we read not only with alert and receptive minds but with feeling hearts as well. E. M. Forster tells us that we ought really to read a book "in two ways at once" so that we are able to follow the writer wherever he wishes to take us; but also, at the end, we should have the shape of the book all in place in our minds, as a structure that we have watched being built before our eyes. We can look at it from every side. We can see what is good about it and what is not.

One who reads a book in this way sees not only the structure of the book, but the idea behind it. The structure is the shape or form the idea takes as it grows in the writer's mind; the way in which he wants to present his idea to the reader. His idea is what he is trying to say, that is, his theme. His medium is language. The quality of the writer's idea, the soundness of the structure he builds, and the expressive power of his language will to a great extent determine the literary quality of his book.

A fine book has something original to say and says it with style. Originality and style are words that are used loosely by many reviewers of books; but, quite simply, an original idea is one that has its origin in the truth as one person sees it, which is never quite the same as anyone else's truth, and so is "original"; a word that is not to be confused with mere novelty.

It should be a simple process to detect a writer who has nothing of his own to say and imitates what he thinks is a successful formula, ignorant of the truth that a secondhand idea is sure to result in a second-rate book; that is, it will lack originality. An original writer will know what he is trying to say because his idea comes from within; it is a fusion of experience, observation, and the creative mind.

Style, on the other hand, describes the different ways writers have of expressing what they want to say. Each one of us forms his sentences differently and the personality of the writer is woven into the manner of his expression. When a writer forms his sentences so that the order and choice of the words is distinguished, he attains literary style. His style, or use of language, is thus both personal and revealing of the quality of the writer.

A good style in writing is not necessarily what is understood as "fine writing," but it should be appropriate to the subject of the book. For example, in such a story as Will James' *Smoky* the writing is appropriate to the story that he tells, because it gives verisimilitude and atmosphere to the particular kind of experience of which Will James writes. It is his personal expression of the subject he has chosen to write about, and the book's value must be judged by considering to what degree his expression has successfully conveyed his original intention or idea.

Choosing a subject for a book is perhaps the least difficult of a writer's problems. He can say, "I will write a book about a circus" or "about a trip to the moon" or "about kindness to animals." The variety of subjects that present themselves seems inexhaustible, and almost any subject may be presented from a variety of points of view. If the writer has nothing of his own to say about the subject, if he has arrived at no personal viewpoint, the book will lack the individuality that only a writer's personal expression can lend it. The result will be a pointless account that lacks impact and challenge, and we say it has no center.

For the subject matter chosen by the writer is there for the purpose of developing his idea, his theme; and takes shape or form as he uses it to construct his book, whether it be fiction or any other form of writing. Variety is one of the characteristics of children's literature. Whatever form a book may have, whether a fairy tale, a book about animals, or the life of a hero, or whatever it may be, it must have some of the qualities inherent in good writing of any kind if it is to deserve serious consideration.

It cannot be claimed, therefore, that books can be placed in order of importance to children according to subject matter; that a biography is more important than a fairy tale. There is an attitude that has some prevalence among adults that informational books are more *valuable* to a child than other kinds because they provide him with the materials of knowledge which will help him to get on in life, forgetting that a child's own curiosity and desire to know and understand make him turn readily and of his own accord to all the sources of information about the things that interest him.

But books of imagination also furnish the mind, if not in so purely utilitarian a fashion. They give it scope and awareness, beauty and growth. Growth comes only through contact with what is larger and greater than oneself—something to "stretch" the mind and give direction to the imagination. Because the books in which the imaginative content is greatest are more closely akin to pure literature and are richer in the qualities that we find in great writing, let us consider from the standpoint of construction, idea, and expression, those books in which the subject matter is treated imaginatively. Of these, the greatest number are fiction. Fiction is also the most difficult of all forms of writing in which to distinguish between what is good and what is not good; between what is significant and what is trivial.

We have said that the writer's idea, the structure he builds, and his power to express his idea in language will to a great extent determine the literary quality of his book. Let us examine these determining qualities in this order, as they apply to fiction for children. In an analysis of fiction, the idea behind the story is our first concern. No story can carry itself unless there is an idea at the back of it, even though it is an obvious or hackneyed one such as "be kind to animals, they are our friends."

Authors of second-rate children's stories too often choose an improving theme. Perhaps it is because their books are written by adults for children, and not, as in general fiction, by adults for other adults. There are many authors who are more anxious to write a story that will support a cause in which they, as adults, are interested rather than to tell a story for the sake of the pleasure it will give to a child.

Ever since there have been books written for children there have been fashions in concepts of what children's books should be. Looking back at the history of forgotten children's books we can recall the emphasis that was placed on making children polite, or pious, or well-informed on every subject, or even on some social or economic aspect of the period with which adults of the time were preoccupied. This was a well-intentioned and sincere effort on the part of those writers whose names are now as forgotten as their books. But their ideas were based on uncritical standards of the nature of literature, and on a complete misconception of the nature of children.

"Grownups," says Paul Hazard, "want to suppress that happy interval of years in which we live without dragging the weight of life about with us, rich years in which our being is not only shaping itself, but receiving in advance its best share of happiness." He then goes on to tell us the kinds of books which seem to him good. "Books that remain faithful to the very essence of art; those that offer to children an intuitive and direct way of knowledge, a simple beauty capable of being perceived immediately, arousing in their souls a vibration which will endure all their lives." He finds good the books "that give them respect for universal life," that "respect the valor and eminent dignity of play; which understand that the training of intelligence and reason cannot, and must not, always have the immediately useful and practical as its goal." He also likes books of knowledge "especially when they distill from all the different kinds of knowledge the most difficult and the most necessary—that of the human heart." "Men," he says, "have always oppressed children," and explains his meaning in one sentence: "But to misshape young souls, to profit by a certain facility that one may possess to add to the number of indigestible and sham books, to give oneself too easily the airs of a moralist and scholar, to cheat in quality, that is what I call oppressing children."[1]

When a new children's book is acclaimed by adults, not because of its creative conception, its imaginative treatment, its values in the art of writing for children, but merely because the subject matter confirms an adult interest in some ephemeral phase of adult problems or experience, it is time to ask oneself whether a new book is being praised for right reasons, or because of mistaken ideas of what constitutes a suitable theme for a good children's book. Helen Haines, in her *What's in a Novel*, says:

> It is strange how many intelligent people whose interest in reading is quite genuine and whose confidence in their own judgment is rarely shaken, remain completely insensitive to the quality of a book as literature; for them the subject and the moral tone are the only things that count.[2]

[1] Paul Hazard, *Books, Children and Men* (Boston: Horn Book, 1944), p.4, 42-44.
[2] Helen E. Haines, *What's in a Novel* (N.Y.: Columbia Univ. Pr., 1942), p.244.

The unreluctant years

The idea, or the theme, of a writer tells us not only what the writer is trying to say in his book, but it also tells us whether it has significance for the reader for whom it was intended. When it is intended for children, they, themselves, will give the final verdict, because children cannot long be deceived by the books to which their instinctive response is not that of their kinship with joy, wonder, and delight.

A theme should be woven into the structure of the book naturally and consistently and should develop with the story—not hammered in, in an obvious way, in isolated incidents. It should be developed through the action or events of the book and through the characters and conversation. To take a simple example: If the theme is "the cunning of the fox," children do not want to be told in a story that the fox is a cunning animal. They want to *see* him showing craft and cunning in the things that happen in the story and so build up their picture of the nature of the fox.

We can imagine that this story of the cunning fox tells of one event after another until the point of climax when, in his highest moment, the fox's cunning triumphs—or else is defeated because his cunning overreaches itself. The rest of the story will bring out the consequences whatever they may be. That is to say, our story will have a beginning, a middle, and an end. The series of events will hold our interest because we can see that each event is leading us to something and we want to go on and find out what happens.

The difference between a narrative of events and a constructed plot is difficult to explain. The best explanation, I think, is given in E. M. Forster's *Aspects of the Novel* in which he says "if it is in a story" (which he defines as "a narrative of events arranged in their time sequence") "we say 'and then?' If it is in a plot we ask 'why?' "[3] He says that "The king died and then the queen died" is a story. "The king died, and then the queen died of grief" is a plot. It is the plot which puts the events of the story in relation to each other and to the story considered as a whole.

The immediate interest of children is in the action of the story the author tells. If it is not a good plot, no matter with what skill or art it is presented, it will not hold their interest for long. At the same time, children recognize a difference in the stories they read, and are aware of other values, when they are present, than those of pure entertainment.

[3] E. M. Forster, *Aspects of the Novel* (N.Y.: Harcourt, 1949), p.82-83.

40

There are stories for children which are purely objective, which rely for their interest on the quick-moving action of the tale. These stories create an atmosphere of suspense. Their interest is centered on the outcome of the imagined events, and, once this is known, the interest drops. The excitement, for the reader, is in proportion to the skill with which the plot is handled, but if suspense is all the book has to offer, there is little pleasure in rereading it since the suspense disappears in a second reading.

There are other objective stories in which, while the action is their immediate attraction, the characters of the story take on life and individuality until they live in the reader's imagination long after the events of the story fade from the mind. A child, for instance, may read a number of stories about pirates and find them more or less equally entertaining. They will leave practically the same impression. But when he reads Stevenson's *Treasure Island* he carries away a distinct idea of having met a terrifying, although somewhat likeable pirate, a living character who, by the alchemy of Stevenson's imagination, will always be to him Long John Silver, the pirate of pirates.

In these stories the writer uses an objective approach to his subject. Everything is there for the sake of the story—the imagined events, the characters who are affected by the events or who bring them about, the setting, or the time and place, in which the events happen. Their place in literature is determined, not by the suspense of the story, but by other factors; the writer's ability to create memorable and living characters, not just puppets or types who are necessary to the action; the writer's sense of place and time which makes the "climate" of the story a pervasive influence within which the reader feels the illusion of reality, not mere scene painting but giving the tale added depth and subtlety; and finally, there is the writer's power of language.

These factors tell us whether a story of this kind is a good story or a poor one, whether it is worth reading more than once or even whether it is worth reading at all. To write an objective story in the way Robert Louis Stevenson has written *Treasure Island* produces a classic of children's literature. In inept hands this method results in sensationalism and mediocrity.

But there is another way of writing for children than the purely objective. There is the story in which we hear overtones and which has values other than those of the events of the story. We feel that the writer is remembering his own childhood and is bringing his mature understanding and experience of life to illuminate an imaginary experience of childhood. His approach is subjective rather than objective. He has something he wants to say to children and charms them into listening through his ability to tell a story.

Paul Hazard asks that children's books contain a profound morality; that they set in action certain truths worthy of lasting forever, that maintain in their own behalf faith in truth and justice. To write for children in this way demands a great deal from the writer; a sense of the importance of universal moral and spiritual values, creative and imaginative powers, and strength of expression, of language. The books of such writers as George Macdonald and W. H. Hudson have this profound significance, this imaginative quality, and creative expression. In less gifted and less mature writers the subjective approach to a children's book can become merely confused, condescending, and trivial.

In appraising the worth of a book as literature it is always well to consider what other books it finds congenial associates. If it keeps good company, if it takes its place naturally in one's mind beside books whose permanent value has been established, it must share some of the qualities those books possess. If, on the other hand, we associate it with more ephemeral and more trivial books, it will be seen to lack the qualities we find in good writing.

The ability to distinguish a good book from a poor one, to know when the spirit of literature is present and when it is not, requires the sensitive feeling and reasoning of the reader which tells him, "This is right" and "this is real," or that it is not. There is no formula we can apply which will infallibly tell us whether what we are reading is good or bad. Familiarity with and understanding of the books which have been proved to have permanent value will give a bedrock of reasoning and feeling which one can work from, and go back to, in the evaluating of contemporary writing for children. For, as Arthur Quiller-Couch says:

> Our trust will in the end repose upon masterpieces, upon the great classics of whatever Language or Literature we are handling: and these, in any language are neither enormous in number and mass, nor extraordinarily difficult to detect, nor (best of all) forbidding to the reader by reason of their own difficulty. Upon a selected few of these—even upon three, or two, or one—we may teach at least a surmise of the true delight, and may be some measure of taste whereby

our pupil will, by an inner guide, be warned to choose the better and reject the worse when we turn him loose to read for himself . . . and it may suffice us that these include Universality and Permanence. Your true classic is *universal,* in that it appeals to the catholic mind of man. It is doubly *permanent:* for it remains significant, or acquires a new significance, after the age for which it was written and the conditions under which it was written, have passed away; and it yet keeps, undefaced by handling, the original noble imprint of the mind that first minted it—or shall we say that, as generation after generation rings the coin, it ever returns the echo of its father-spirit?[4]

ASSOCIATIVE READING

HAINES, HELEN. Reviewing a Novel (in *What's in a Novel*). Columbia Univ. Pr., 1942.

HAZARD, PAUL. Books, Children and Men, tr. from the French by Margaret Mitchell. Horn Book, 1944.

LOWES, JOHN LIVINGSTON. Of Reading Books. Houghton, Mifflin, 1929. Constable, 1930.

MOORE, ANNE CARROLL, and MILLER, BERTHA MAHONY, eds. Writing and Criticism; a Book for Margery Bianco. Horn Book, 1951.

MOORE, ANNIE EGERTON. Literature Old and New for Children, Materials for a College Course. Houghton, Mifflin, 1934.

QUILLER-COUCH, Sir ARTHUR THOMAS. On the Art of Reading. Putnam, 1925. Cambridge Univ. Pr., 1920.

——. On the Art of Writing. Putnam, 1916. Cambridge Univ. Pr., 1916.

SWINNERTON, FRANK ARTHUR. The Reviewing and Criticism of Books. Dent, 1939.

WOOLF, VIRGINIA. How Should One Read a Book (in *Second Common Reader*). Harcourt, Brace, 1932.

[4] Sir Arthur Quiller-Couch, *On the Art of Reading* (London: Cambridge Univ. Pr., 1920), p.198-99.

CHAPTER FOUR

My impression is that people in fairy tales behave pretty much as people do in real life. Some live by high principles, some are given over to evil ways; some are kindly in disposition, others practice meanness and persecution. Some go adventuring, some stay at home. There are strong and weak people, honest and devious people, people with great intelligence, and many with little or none. And in fairy tales each type, with the action that represents it, is brought to life objectively, emphatically and consistently. Fairy tales do not "condone" behavior that is contrary to ethical principle. They simply recognize the fact that it occurs.

Annis Duff,
Bequest of Wings

THE ART OF THE FAIRY TALE

 Fairy tales, as a form of fiction, have almost no place in the reading of adults. Yet everyone has heard or read fairy tales in childhood, and a more universal reading interest among children would be hard to find. That fairy tales have a permanent place in children's literature may be assumed, since a story which has lived for hundreds of years must possess a vitality which is imperishable and immutable.

Like all traditional literature, fairy tales were originally the possession of everyone, adults and children alike. They were preserved and used and valued by the common folk from the time of the childhood of the human race. They still survived in their original form in remote and isolated places until the work of scholars, who wrote them down from word of mouth, preserved these tales for all time in printed books.

Why did scholars such as Asbjørnsen and Moe and the brothers Grimm spend years of their lives in searching out and collecting these original folk tales? It is certain that they were not seeking to confer a benefit on children's literature, although this they have unwittingly done. They were concerned not in the fairy tales as stories but in the light these old tales could throw on the customs and beliefs of early times and, through comparison of variants of the same tale, with the migrations of the Aryan family. It is not, however, because of their interest to students but because of their inherent qualities as literature that these traditional stories hold so important a place in the reading of children.

Traditional is a word we apply to stories and verse whose origin is lost in the mists of time. No one knows their authors nor when or where they were first told. They seem to be as old as the race itself. Many scholarly treatises have been written on the history of folk literature, and any interested person can find such source material readily at hand. But our concern is with the fairy tale as it exists today, what its claim is to consideration as literature, and what is its value and interest for children.

Although adults have discarded fairy tales in their own reading, judging them childishly fanciful, unreal, and unrelated to the world as they know it—a world in which the workings of natural law are familiar and accepted—it is remarkable how many references to fairy tales are found in adult speech and writing. We all understand the implication of such phrases as it's a Cinderella tale; he's an Ugly Duckling; he killed the goose that laid the golden egg; it's a case of Beauty and the Beast; a veritable Bluebeard; Sister Ann, Sister Ann do you see any one coming; Open Sesame; an old man of the sea; and many others. These allusions in common speech testify to the memorable quality of fairy tales. But do they not also in some sort refute the judgment of grownups that these stories are unrelated to everyday life? Let us look at them more closely, approaching them without prejudice as we would a contemporary volume. What do we find?

Here is a story which we call a fairy tale, although there are no fairies among the characters. In its native German it is one of the *Märchen* collected by the Grimm brothers, but since we have no equivalent in English for the term *Märchen* we sometimes find it translated as "household stories," or "folk tales." These terms describe a traditional story in which ordinary people in all conditions of life live in a world in which extraordinary happenings occur. Let us read this story and discover, if we can, what its claims are to literature, and its particular value as literature for children.

> In times past there lived a king and queen, who said to each other every day of their lives, "Would that we had a child!" and yet they had none. But it happened once that when the queen was bathing, there came a frog out of the water, and he squatted on the ground, and said to her,
>
> "Thy wish shall be fulfilled; before a year has gone by, thou shalt bring a daughter into the world."
>
> And as the frog foretold, so it happened; and the queen bore a daughter so beautiful that the king could not contain himself for joy, and he ordained a great feast. Not only did he bid to it his relations, friends, and acquaintances, but also the wise women, that they might be kind and favourable to the child. There were thirteen

of them in his kingdom, but as he had only provided twelve golden plates for them to eat from, one of them had to be left out. However, the feast was celebrated with all splendour; and as it drew to an end, the wise women stood forward to present to the child their wonderful gifts: one bestowed virtue, one beauty, a third riches, and so on, whatever there is in the world to wish for. And when eleven of them had said their say, in came the uninvited thirteenth, burning to revenge herself, and without greeting or respect, she cried with a loud voice,

"In the fifteenth year of her age the princess shall prick herself with a spindle and shall fall down dead."

And without speaking one more word she turned away and left the hall. Every one was terrified at her saying, when the twelfth came forward, for she had not yet bestowed her gift, and though she could not do away with the evil prophecy, yet she could soften it, so she said,

"The princess shall not die, but fall into a deep sleep for a hundred years."

Now the king, being desirous of saving his child even from this misfortune, gave commandment that all the spindles in his kingdom should be burnt up.

The maiden grew up, adorned with all the gifts of the wise women; and she was so lovely, modest, sweet, and kind and clever, that no one who saw her could help loving her.

It happened one day, she being already fifteen years old, that the king and queen rode abroad, and the maiden was left behind alone in the castle. She wandered about into all the nooks and corners, and into all the chambers and parlours, as the fancy took her, till at last she came to an old tower. She climbed the narrow winding stair which led to a little door, with a rusty key sticking out of the lock; she turned the key, and the door opened, and there in the little room sat an old woman with a spindle, diligently spinning her flax.

"Good day, mother," said the princess, "what are you doing?"

"I am spinning," answered the old woman, nodding her head.

"What thing is that that twists round so briskly?" asked the maiden, and taking the spindle into her hand she began to spin; but no sooner had she touched it than the evil prophecy was fulfilled, and she pricked her finger with it. In that very moment she fell back upon the bed that stood there, and lay in a deep sleep. And this sleep fell upon the whole castle; the king and queen, who had returned and were in the great hall, fell fast asleep, and with them the whole court. The horses in their stalls, the dogs in the yard, the pigeons on the roof, the flies on the wall, the very fire that flickered on the hearth, became still, and slept like the rest; and the meat on the spit ceased roasting, and the cook, who was going to pull the scullion's hair for some mistake he had made, let him go, and went to sleep. And the wind ceased, and not a leaf fell from the trees about the castle.

Then round about that place there grew a hedge of thorns thicker every year, until at last the whole castle was hidden from view, and nothing of it could be seen but the vane on the roof. And a rumour went abroad in all that country of the beautiful sleeping Rosamond, for so was the princess called; and from time to time many kings' sons came and tried to force their way through the hedge; but it was impossible for them to do so, for the thorns held fast together like strong hands, and the young men were caught by them, and not being able to get free, there died a lamentable death.

Many a long year afterwards there came a king's son into that country, and heard an old man tell how there should be a castle standing behind the hedge of thorns, and that there a beautiful enchanted princess named Rosamond had slept for a hundred years, and with her the king and queen, and the whole court. The old man had been told by his grandfather that many kings' sons had sought to pass the thorn-hedge, but had been caught and pierced by the thorns and had died a miserable death. Then said the young man, "Nevertheless, I do not fear to try; I shall win through and see the lovely Rosamond." The good old man tried to dissuade him, but he would not listen to his words.

For now the hundred years were at an end, and the day had come when Rosamond should be awakened. When the prince drew near the hedge of thorns, it was changed into a hedge of beautiful large flowers, which parted and bent aside to let him pass, and then closed behind him in a thick hedge. When he reached the castle-yard, he saw the horses and brindled hunting-dogs lying asleep, and on the roof the pigeons were sitting with their heads under their wings. And when he came indoors, the flies on the wall were asleep, the cook in the kitchen had his hand uplifted to strike the scullion, and the kitchen-maid had the black fowl on her lap ready to pluck. Then he mounted higher, and saw in the hall the whole court lying asleep, and above them, on their thrones, slept the king and the queen. And still he went farther, and all was so quiet that he could hear his own breathing; and at last he came to the tower, and went up the winding stair, and opened the door of the little room where Rosamond

48

lay. And when he saw her looking so lovely in her sleep, he could not turn away his eyes; and presently he stooped and kissed her, and she awaked, and opened her eyes, and looked very kindly on him. And she rose, and they went forth together, and the king and the queen and whole court waked up, and gazed on each other with great eyes of wonderment. And the horses in the yard got up and shook themselves, the hounds sprang up and wagged their tails, the pigeons on the roof drew their heads from under their wings, looked round, and flew into the field, the flies on the wall crept on a little farther, the kitchen fire leapt up and blazed, and cooked the meat, the joint on the spit began to roast, the cook gave the scullion such a box on the ear that he roared out, and the maid went on plucking the fowl.

Then the wedding of the Prince and Rosamond was held with all splendour, and they lived very happily together until their lives' end.[1]

The idea of this tale is familiar to us. We have met it before in the Greek myth of Persephone and in the Northern story of Brunhilde left to sleep encircled with a hedge of flames. All these stories suggest the theme of the long sleep of winter and the awakening of spring.

The convention within which the story is told is also familiar to us. There is the husband and wife (in this case a king and queen) who wish for a child; the prophecy concerning the fulfillment of their wish foretold by supernatural means (the frog who appears when the queen is bathing); the feast in honor of the child to which are invited twelve wise women who bestow their fairy gifts; and the uninvited thirteenth who wreaks vengeance for this slight by dooming the princess to death. But the dismay of all is allayed by a still further gift that softens the doom of death to a long sleep. The climax is reached when everything happens as foretold and the castle with all it contains falls into its hundred years' sleep. Then with the coming of the prince and the awakening kiss, in true fairy tale tradition "they lived happily ever after."

The conventional form of the story makes the denouement a fore-gone conclusion to seasoned readers of fairy tales, and we ask ourselves in what lies the interest and perennial freshness the story undeniably has. Consider in the first place the romantic situation the story presents: a beautiful princess possessed of "whatever there is in the world

[1] Jakob and Wilhelm Grimm, "The Sleeping Beauty," in their *Household Stories* (N.Y.: Macmillan, 1923).

to wish for" and yet, through the action of cruel spite, doomed to lose it all. Our concern is centered on that future moment. How will it come about, since a father's care has removed, seemingly, the means of threatened danger? It happens quite naturally when the princess, left alone one day, wanders about the castle in search of diversion and comes to an old tower. "She climbed the narrow winding stair which led to a little door" and behind that door, in the little tower room, "as was foretold, so it happened." At the same moment that the evil prophecy is fulfilled and the princess falls asleep, the whole castle falls under the same spell. The tale pictures the scene vividly even to the flies on the wall and "the very fire that flickered on the hearth, became still, and slept." There is pictured, too, the hedge of thorns thickening about the castle until it is hidden from view. Only the legend told in the countryside reminds the curious of the sleeping princess. It brings many kings' sons to try to make their way through the hedge and who there die "a lamentable death."

But now the hundred years are fulfilled and another king's son makes the attempt and wins through. We see him entering the court-yard and the palace. Precisely the same scene is again described that we saw taking place a hundred years before, until he comes at last to the tower room. "And when he saw her looking so lovely in her sleep, he could not turn away his eyes; and presently he stooped and kissed her, and she awaked." At this moment, just as everything and everyone went to sleep at the same time, so now the castle awakes with the princess. But the third repetition of the description is in reverse—as if we had watched a clock run down and stop, and then the clock still stopped after long years, and lastly, the clock begins to tick again as if it had never stopped.

This repetitive description, slightly varied in each case, has a significance in the structure of the story. It gives emphasis and continuity to the central idea, the castle held in its long sleep. It also gives unity to the two parts of the story, the fulfilling of the evil prophecy and the coming of the liberator. We can see the effectiveness of the idea or theme of the story and we can recognize the skill with which it is constructed. Let us look at the language of the story and see if we cannot discover another reason why it has lived as long as the race has endured.

Notice the diction and the rhythm of the phrasing. The language of the narrative has the dignity and simplicity we find in all great litera-

50

ture—in the parables of the Bible, for example, since the essential truth presented in this story (that though evil may prevail over good for a time, love must in the end triumph over evil) is analogous to the truth inherent in the parables. Notice too the restraint with which the incidents are related. "The queen bore a daughter so beautiful that the king could not contain himself for joy." But it is left to the reader to supply the details of in what her beauty consisted. And again "the feast was celebrated with all splendour," but that is all we are told of its wonders, though the "golden plates," the insufficient supply of which brought about the catastrophic ending of the feast, lend color to our imagination.

There is not an unnecessary word to impede the direct and forceful telling of the story. It flows in rhythmical sentences, unencumbered by explanatory or descriptive phrases, until the princess pricks her finger and falls asleep. At this point, note the concrete detail which describes how sleep fell upon the whole castle, how the life and activity and bustle changed in the flick of an eyelid into the stillness of stone. There is humor in the cook's uplifted hand caught and held as he is about to pull the scullion's hair. There is poetry in the final sentence of this description that sets the mood of the sleeping castle: "And the wind ceased, and not a leaf fell from the trees about the castle." No wonder the story is timeless. It is romance and adventure in a form that a child understands and responds to. It is told with beauty and imagination. It touches art at every point.

Children read "The Sleeping Beauty" and other fairy tales because they are good stories, but it is not the story interest alone that enthralls. Through a fairy tale, a child enters another world—a world of wonder—which is like, and yet surprisingly unlike, the world he knows. Here, almost anything can, and does, happen. As Walter de la Mare tells us:

> Above all, it must be remembered that however real and actual the characters, scenes and events may seem to us as we read, these are tales of the *imagination*. Up to a point and within their own framework they are reasonable enough; but it is a wild reasonableness. Whether we can accept what they tell us, whether we delight in them or not, depends then, on how much imagination we have ourselves. It would be merely ridiculous to say that such and such a thing couldn't have happened. It is a world imagined and it is made to happen there.[2]

[2] Walter de la Mare, *Animal Stories* (N.Y.: Scribner, 1940), p.xxxviii.

51

The unreluctant years

There is, in fairy tales, a general tone, a pervasive atmosphere, of marvellous happenings. Related in a natural and even matter-of-fact way, they satisfy the imagination of children with their dramatic completeness, their exciting incidents, their humor and romance in a marvellous world.

Fairy tales have other values in children's reading than as stories and as food for the imagination. These tales have come down through the centuries from the *folk*, from primitive peoples. Inherent in them are many of the characteristics of the later literature of the country of their origin. In Grimm's *Household Tales* we find the stoic German character, its love of homely detail and incident, its down-to-earth practical attitude toward life, its inventive spirit. In Perrault's *Fairy Tales* there is the clarity and the light touch that is almost offhand, the logical working out of events, the adroit manner and quick wit shown in overcoming difficulties characteristic of the French. In Jacob's *English Fairy Tales* we find the basic common sense and terseness of the Anglo-Saxon, the understatement which is their humor, and we find too their love of freedom and fair play. In Dasent's *Tales from the Norse* he himself characterizes their quality as "bold and humorous, in the true sense of humour. In the midst of every difficulty and danger arises that old Norse feeling of *making the best of everything, and keeping a good face to the foe.*"

These stories reflect their origin, the qualities and atmosphere of the country from which they came. The differences that natural environment and racial character make in the development of imaginative literature may be seen in a comparison of the fairy tales of, for instance, Norway and France. Here, for example, is one of the best known stories from the Norse, the excellent tale of "The Three Billy Goats Gruff":

> Once on a time there were three billy-goats, who were to go up to the hillside to make themselves fat, and the name of all three was "Gruff."
>
> On the way up was a bridge over a stream they had to cross, and under the bridge lived a great ugly Troll, with eyes as big as saucers, and a nose as long as a poker.
>
> So first of all came the youngest billy-goat Gruff to cross the bridge.
>
> "Trip, trap; trip, trap," went the bridge.
>
> "Who's that tripping over my bridge?" roared the Troll.
>
> "Oh, it is only I, the tiniest billy-goat Gruff, and I'm going up to

the hillside to make myself fat," said the billy-goat, with such a small voice.

"Now, I'm coming to gobble you up," said the Troll.

"Oh no, pray don't take me. I'm too little, that I am," said the billy-goat; "wait a bit till the second billy-goat Gruff comes—he's much bigger."

"Well, be off with you," said the Troll.

A little while after came the second billy-goat Gruff to cross the bridge.

"Trip, trap! trip, trap! trip, trap!" went the bridge.

"WHO'S THAT tripping over my bridge?" roared the Troll.

"Oh, it's the second billy-goat Gruff, and I'm going up to the hillside to make myself fat," said the billy-goat, who hadn't such a small voice.

"Now, I'm coming to gobble you up," said the Troll.

"Oh no, don't take me; wait a little till the big billy-goat Gruff comes—he's much bigger."

"Very well; be off with you," said the Troll.

But just then up came the big billy-goat Gruff.

"TRIP, TRAP! TRIP, TRAP! TRIP, TRAP! TRIP, TRAP!" went the bridge, for the billy-goat was so heavy that the bridge creaked and groaned under him.

"WHO'S THAT tramping over my bridge?" roared the Troll.

"IT'S I—THE BIG BILLY-GOAT GRUFF," said the billy-goat, who had an ugly hoarse voice of his own.

"Now, I'm coming to gobble you up!" roared the Troll.

> "Well, come along! I've got two spears,
> And I'll poke your eyeballs out at your ears;
> I've got besides two curling-stones,
> And I'll crush you to bits, body and bones."

That was what the big billy-goat said; and so he flew at the Troll and poked his eyes out with his horns, and crushed him to bits, body and bones, and tossed him out into the stream, and after that he went up to the hillside. There the billy-goats got so fat they were scarce able to walk home again; and if the fat hasn't fallen off them, why they're still fat; and so:

> "Snip, snap, snout,
> This tale's told out."[3]

Notice the brevity with which the story is told. No details are given

---

[3] Peter Christen Asbjørnsen, *East of the Sun and West of the Moon* (N.Y.: Macmillan, 1928), p.31.

except those which concern the story itself. It is reduced to the barest essentials. Yet within its action are shown the environment and the native character which give it a distinctive Norse feeling. The story suggests, but does not describe, the headlong mountain stream rushing under the bridge which gives passage to the steep spruce-clad hillside beyond. The bold, sturdy, headstrong attributes of the characters of the story harmonize with the setting and with our conception of the Norse character. The supernatural element introduced in the Troll suggests the menace ever present in the rushing waters under the bridge, for it is a country where nature holds danger for the unwary.

The form of the story has the terseness, simplicity, and vigor of the best folk tales; a form which has the strength, objectiveness, and restraint that we look for in all good writing. Constant repetition through the ages has developed and preserved the effective way of telling the story; only the needful and appropriate words remain.

A device used in folk tales to heighten the effect is the repetition of both incident and phrase. This device is an accepted and familiar one, and is found in many stories such as "The Three Little Pigs" and "The Three Bears." The charm of this type of tale lies in the fact that each incident, while like the others, varies slightly with each recital. In this way the now familiar steps in the story each serve as a foil to the introduction of something new.

This use of repetition with variation provides mounting interest and expectation on the part of the reader or listener. In "The Three Billy Goats Gruff," the building up of the action toward a sudden and effective climax is entirely satisfying and skilful. The comparative dimensions of the three billy-goats have their parallel in the increasing volume in the sound of their feet on the bridge. This is further accentuated by the repetitive phrase "Trip, trap," twice for "the tiniest," three times for "the second" and four times for "the big" billy-goat Gruff. It also repeats itself in the form in which the Troll roars his challenge to each of the goats:

TO FIRST GOAT: "Who's that tripping?"
TO SECOND GOAT: *"Who's that* tripping?"
TO THIRD GOAT: *"Who's that tramping?"*

There is a well-rounded, artistic pattern in the return to the original purpose of the three billy-goats Gruff "to go up the hillside" which is accomplished in the concluding paragraph. The nonsense rhyme which ends it all with the right flourish is evidently a traditional Norse ending. A slightly different version of the rhyme is found in "Katie Woodencloak"—a longer and more elaborate tale:

> Snip, snap, snover,
> This story's over.

But the one-syllable words of

> Snip, snap, snout,
> This tale's told out

is in keeping with the terse telling of "The Three Billy Goats Gruff."

All the essentials of a good short story may be found in this Norse folk tale: an arresting opening, dramatic action, suspense, dramatic climax, and a well-rounded ending. As an expression of the mind and temperament of the Norse folk, it has simplicity and strength, humor and a valorous spirit. It is a picture painted with bold, rhythmic strokes in primary colors, clear and invigorating as the air and contour of the Norseland itself.

Turning from the Norse to the fairy tales of France we find that the shaping spirit of the French literary genius gives these stories as marked a national character as those of the Norse. If we look briefly at Perrault's version of "Puss in Boots" it will be seen that the charm of the story is at least partly dependent on the character of Puss in Boots himself. The other figures in the story are mere types. But the cat who at the beginning of the story had, at most, only a reputation for cleverness in catching mice and rats, not only makes the fortune of the miller's son, but shows himself to be quick-witted and inventive, brave enough to take risks for his master, and adroit in the use of flattery. Yet in essence he remains a cat, and when, with exquisite courtesy and adroit flattery, he persuades the ogre to take the form of a mouse, he "did the very best a cat can do, and the most natural under the circumstances, he sprang upon the mouse and gobbled it up in a trice."

The tone of the story is that of a calm acceptance of remarkable events, recounted in a seemingly direct, even matter-of-fact way, yet with a half-ironic and amused undertone. And it is this undertone that is the keynote to the charm and mood of the story—light, graceful, and gay. The debonair "Puss in Boots" is as French in style and mood as "The Three Billy Goats Gruff" is typically Norse.

The universal appeal of the fairy tale has led to a multiplicity of versions for children. But the folk tales of individual peoples are of little value as literature if they only repeat the external events of the stories in undistinguished language. They must also preserve the feeling of the culture and environment of the people from which they have come if children are not to be the losers in their reading of fairy tales. For the part that fairy tales play in children's literary and imaginative development is precisely that of any other literary art form. Fairy tales are anonymous, but those which originated among a people with a genius for literary creation are the product of a true art impulse. Faithfulness to this art form should be preserved in the versions given to children. Annie E. Moore writes, in *Literature Old and New for Children*:

> Literary critics [use fairy tales] as striking examples of story construction, dramatic quality, pervading tone, character delineation, clarity of theme, intensity of action, effective dialogue, and other significant traits . . . because the best of these tales exhibit striking qualities free from the complexities of a more sophisticated literature. The student of children's literature should be no less aware of the factors which contribute to the excellence of stories which long since became the especial property of the young.[4]

In reading versions of the same story, we find they vary widely in expression even while the events are the same. This is sometimes due to a modern reteller's view that the folk language preserved in earlier versions is archaic and so is unsuited to present-day children.

In evaluating a new version which uses modern colloquial expressions in place of the folk language of traditional versions, we must ask ourselves whether greater clarity and simplicity is really achieved through the use of modern colloquialisms and undistinguished language. We must ask, too, if the modern version does not sacrifice the smooth, rhythmic style which makes the older version a pleasure to the ear, with no awkward constructions and obtrusive words to interrupt the musical flow of the story.

It is necessary to remember that the fairy tale has come down to us as an art form in style and technique. The version, modern or traditional, given to children should be the one which best transmits the quality of "artless art" in the original folk tales, which to the Grimm brothers were "brimming over with life and beauty and imagination."

[4] Annie E. Moore, *Literature Old and New for Children* (Boston: Houghton, Mifflin, 1934), p.95-96.

The more fairy tales we read the more difficult we find it to make generalizations about stories of such variety of theme and content, structure and expression. Each fairy tale is a narrative which stands or falls on its own merits and must be analyzed as a piece of writing as well as for the factors which endear it to children as a story. Various though fairy tales are, they have certain characteristics in common which we come to expect and look for. There is a generally accepted idea, for instance, that all fairy tales begin with the words "once upon a time" and end with the familiar conclusion "so they lived happily ever after." Some fairy tales do begin and end this way, but many do not. Yet this characteristic beginning and ending is implied in almost all these stories even when they begin and end without them. That is to say, they begin simply, they come to the point with brevity, they give only the facts which concern the action of the story, and the ending follows swiftly and conclusively. Let us look at the way in which some of the most familiar stories begin:

> An old woman was sweeping her house, and she found a little crooked sixpence. "What," said she, "shall I do with this little sixpence? I will go to market, and buy a little pig."
>
> As she was coming home, she came to a stile: but the pig would not go over the stile.

> One day Henny-Penny was picking up corn in the cornyard when —whack!—something hit her upon the head. "Goodness gracious me!" said Henny-Penny; "the sky's a-going to fall; I must go and tell the king."

> Mr. and Mrs. Vinegar lived in a vinegar bottle. Now, one day when Mr. Vinegar was from home, Mrs. Vinegar, who was a very good housewife, was busily sweeping her house, when an unlucky thump brought the whole house clitter-clatter, clitter-clatter, about her ears.

How tersely the setting is given for the tale that is to be told, yet how clearly, so that in two or three opening sentences we have before us the chief characters, the place, and the situation from which the action of the story must proceed. The basis of the tale is a simple experience—the finding of a crooked sixpence—a whack on the head of a kernel of corn—the thump of a broom which broke a vinegar bottle. The effect of these beginnings is that we are drawn immediately into the story as if we were there and saw it happen. We ask "What will happen next?" Interest, concern, and suspense are achieved at the very start.

The endings of the fairy tales have a characteristic similarity which is conveyed by the familiar "happy ever after" termination. Fairy tales may indeed end with these words; many of them do. But, whatever the words, the sense of finality, of having satisfactorily disposed of the characters of the story, is as complete as

> Snip, snap, snout,
> This tale's told out.

If we look at a few of the concluding sentences of well-known fairy tales we can see how this finality is achieved:

> From that time forward the robbers never ventured to that house, and the four Bremen town musicians found themselves so well off where they were, that there they stayed. And the last person who related this tale is still living, you see.

> "Then perhaps your name is Rumpelstiltskin!"
> "The devil told you that! the devil told you that!" cried the little man, and in his anger he stamped with his right foot so hard that it went into the ground above his knee; then he seized his left foot with both his hands in such a fury that he split in two, and there was an end of him.

> The Marquis, with a profound bow, accepted the honour that the King had offered him, and that very day he married the Princess. The Cat became a great lord, and he never chased mice afterward except in the way of sport.

A further characteristic of fairy tales is that the same patterns recur. There are many fairy tales, for instance, in which a man, who may be a woodcutter, a miller, or a king, has three sons who set out to seek their fortune. Every child who reads or hears such a tale recognizes its similarity to other already familiar stories. He knows that success will invariably await the youngest son, even though he be thought a simpleton, and so the reader settles down to see how this particular hero will acquit himself.

The recurrence of the pattern of three is another characteristic of these tales: three sons, three daughters, three adventures, three tasks, three suitors, three gifts, three wishes, three riddles. Even the repetition of phrasing is often a pattern of three as in the thrice repeated question and answer

> "Little pig, Little pig, let me come in."
> "No, no, by the hair of my chiny chin chin."

or the admonition "Be bold, be bold," written successively over Mr. Fox's gateway, over his doorway and finally over the dread door in the gallery:

> Be bold, be bold, but not too bold,
> Lest that your heart's blood should run cold.

The heart's blood does sometimes run cold when, as in the story "Mr. Fox," dark deeds and evil doers may alarm and even shock the reader. No advocate of fairy tales as a rich and essential part of children's literature denies the need for a reasonable and wise selection among the large and often unwieldy mass of folk material. But such selections have been made and are readily available—selections which keep in mind the wide variety in taste and temperament between individual children.

From time to time criticisms have been leveled at incidents found in fairy tales which are termed "brutal" without giving consideration either to a child's attitude toward such incidents, or to the manner in which they are presented. Both the child's attitude and the characteristic narrative methods of the folk tale have an impersonal quality important to remember. In the telling it is a matter of emphasis and intention; in the listener, the child, it is a recognition that the events all belong to the realm of story, of imagination. This tacit understanding between narrator and listener induces the appropriate climate in which the events take place. That is to say, in the realm of the fairy tale there is an accepted convention between the teller and the listener.

The story of "Mr. Fox" will serve as an example of this particular kind of story. The heroine discovers the "bravest and most gallant" of her suitors to be a cruel and brutal betrayer of "beautiful young maidens." She outwits and unmasks him. That is the bald outline of the story in terms of actuality, but such a statement gives no clue to the atmosphere and quality of the fairy tale.

With the opening sentences the child is immediately transported from the land of here and now. "Lady Mary was young and Lady Mary was fair. She had two brothers and more lovers than she could count." The reader is in a familiar world, a world which gives him the happy pleasure of recognition as the pattern of events is unrolled, often in precisely repeated terms:

> Be bold, be bold, but not too bold
>
> It is not so, nor it was not so,
> And God forbid it should be so.
>
> But it is so, and it was so,
> Here's hand and ring I have to show.

A quality in things, an atmosphere larger than life is created. The concern is not with individual problems or suffering, but with the abstractions of good and evil and their perpetual conflict told in a story of mounting suspense. The emphasis is not so much on Mr. Fox's wickedness as on the manner of his downfall. The tone is matter-of-fact. And there is no lingering over Mr. Fox's retribution. The moment the pattern of the tale has been worked out, his end is swift, final, and completely impersonal: "At once her brothers and her friends drew their swords and cut Mr. Fox into a thousand pieces."

The child who listens, or reads, has had the pleasure of suspense which heightens the satisfaction of an appropriate conclusion. He has had as well, though he may not know it, the aesthetic pleasure which pattern and form and proportion give, and the moral pleasure of seeing good overcome evil. He has heard simple words used with beauty and skill. These qualities make "Mr. Fox" more than a mere tale of brutal incident. This enlargement of life, characteristic of the fairy tale, is necessary to children, native to them, part of their apprehension of all experience. It is not an attitude created by fairy tales, but rather fairy tales set forth, in terms of art, those ideas and imaginings which already occupy the child's mind.

Against the limitless terrors of a child's own imaginings are set the limits imposed by the convention of the fairy tale. Through a succession of clear mental pictures a child sees that even the weakest can be more than a match for the evil and ugly things in the world if he possess courage, quick wits, and a good heart—a useful and sustaining reflection for anyone in a world as alarming as our own.

In his introduction to *Animal Stories*, Walter de la Mare relates his own experience with such tales when a small child.

> Not all good stories are gay stories. . . . So with a sorrowful, a tragic, even a terrifying tale, picture or poem. That too may feed the imagination, enlighten the mind, strengthen the heart, show us

ourselves. It may grieve, alarm or even shock us, and still remain intensely interesting. Of its own grace and truth and value it will also comfort and console us—with what it recalls to memory of life itself, with what it creates in our minds, with the things, the scenes, the people in it; by the manner in which it reveals itself and its deeper meanings, by its very beauty and verbal music. . . .

. . . A very small boy may go shivering to bed after listening to the teeny tiny tale of the teeny tiny little woman who found a teeny tiny little bone in the churchyard. The very marrow in his bones may tremble at that final "TAKE IT!" Mine used to; and yet I delighted to have it told me again and again by my mother. Some stories, on the other hand, are a little too much for me even at my age. Much depends on how they have been told, and with what reason and intention. Still, even in my youngest days, I could easily manage to stare into Bluebeard's silent and dreadful cupboard, could watch the nail-pierced barrel containing the wicked queen go rolling down a steep place into the sea, and Great Claus's execution with his club. I could dance with Morgiana from oil-jar to oil-jar as she dispatched the Forty Thieves; listen entranced to Falada's head, nailed up on the arch over the gateway, lamenting the misfortunes of his beloved mistress; gasp at the preparation of the ghastly soup in "The Juniper Tree"—and read on. I *enjoyed* these stories, knowing them to be stories, and I am as certain as can be that they did me not the least harm. On the other hand, I can recall one or two tales, of a different kind from these, which I detested, and still detest—anything concerned with deliberate cruelty, for instance. So far as I can remember, not one of these was a folk tale.[5]

But if there are fairy tales that awaken pity and terror, there are also those that kindle wonder and imagination, beauty and poetry. In turning from one kind of fairy tale to another a child finds, in their variety, a deepening and broadening of emotional sympathy. The child's response to suspense, surprise, laughter, sadness, beauty, whatever it may be testifies to the essential rightness and truth of the fairy tale. "Let us never forget that lovely subtle story of bygone days," Paul Hazard says in speaking of the tale of "Beauty and the Beast," in which ugliness is but a spell, broken at last by love and pity.

The beauty and poetry to be found in fairy tales is not only in their deeper meaning, but also in the manner of their telling, the music and rhythm of words. In the *Russian Wonder Tales* we read:

[5] De la Mare, *op. cit.,* p.xviii-xxi.

She walked and walked, whether for a short time or a long time the telling is easy but the journey is not soon done. She wandered for a day and a night, for a week, for two months and for three. She wore through one pair of the iron shoes, and broke to pieces one of the iron staves, and gnawed away one of the stone church-loaves, when, in the midst of a wood which grew always thicker and darker, she came to a lawn. On the lawn was a little hut on whose doorstep sat a sour-faced old woman.

"Whither dost thou hold thy way, beautiful maiden?" asked the old woman.

"O Grandmother," answered the girl, "I beg for thy kindness! Be my hostess and cover me from the dark night. I am searching for Finist the swift bright Falcon, who was my friend."[6]

Or there is the cadence of the recurring verse in "The Black Bull of Norroway"

> "Far have I sought for thee,
> Long have I wrought for thee,
> Near am I brought to thee,
> Dear Duke o' Norroway
> Wilt thou say naught to me—"

Or, as in the opening paragraphs of "The Frog Prince," there is not only the simple beauty of language and the rhythm of sentence structure, but the poetry and charm of word painting as picture succeeds picture:

In the old times, when it was still of some use to wish for the thing one wanted, there lived a King whose daughters were all handsome, but the youngest was so beautiful that the sun himself, who has seen so much, wondered each time he shone over her because of her beauty. Near the royal castle there was a great dark wood, and in the wood under an old linden-tree was a well; and when the day was hot, the King's daughter used to go forth into the wood and sit by the brink of the cool well, and if the time seemed long, she would take out a golden ball, and throw it up and catch it again, and this was her favourite pastime.

Now it happened one day that the golden ball, instead of falling back into the maiden's little hand which had sent it aloft, dropped to the ground near the edge of the well and rolled in. The King's daughter followed it with her eyes as it sank, but the well was deep,

[6] Post Wheeler, "Finist the Falcon," in his *Russian Wonder Tales* (N.Y.: Beechhurst, 1948).

so deep that the bottom could not be seen. Then she began to weep, and she wept and wept as if she could never be comforted. And in the midst of her weeping she heard a voice saying to her,

"What ails thee, King's daughter? Thy tears would melt a heart of stone."

And when she looked to see where the voice came from, there was nothing but a frog stretching his thick ugly head out of the water.

Examples such as these are plentiful in the folklore of those races whose stories grew out of a genuine art impulse. But we must remember that all peoples have not this genius for literary creation. The folk lore of a people without it will be of interest to the student or collector of folk tales, but as literature for children such stories have slight, if any, value merely because they are old. They must also have the inherent qualities of literature. They must possess the active, dramatic ingredients of a good story if they are to stand beside the old favorites in the literature of fairy tales, the stories to which children return again and again because of their perennial freshness and imaginative power.

ASSOCIATIVE READING

BUCHAN, JOHN. The Novel and the Fairy Tale. Oxford Univ. Pr., 1931. (English Association Pamphlet no. 79)

CHESTERTON, G. K. The Dragon's Grandmother (in *Tremendous Trifles*). Dodd, 1909. Methuen, 1909.

———. The Red Angel (in *Tremendous Trifles*). Dodd, 1909. Methuen, 1909.

HARTLAND, EDWIN SIDNEY. The Science of Fairy Tales. Scribner, 1925. Methuen, 1925.

HOOKER, B. Narrative and the Fairy Tale. *Bookman*, XXXIII (June, July 1911), 389-93, 501-05.

———. Types of Fairy Tales. *Forum*, XL (October 1908), 375-84.

REPPLIER, AGNES. The Battle of the Babes (in *Essays in Miniature*). Houghton, Mifflin, 1895.

CHAPTER FIVE

*And he sang of the birth of Time, and of the heavens and the dancing stars;
and of the ocean, and the ether; and the fire, and the shaping of the
wondrous earth. And he sang of the treasures of the hills, and the
hidden jewels of the mine, and the veins of fire and metal, and the
virtues of all healing herbs, and of the speech of birds, and of
prophecy, and of hidden things to come.*

*Then he sang of health, and strength, and manhood and a valiant
heart; and of music, and hunting, and wrestling, and all the games
which heroes love; and of travel, and wars, and sieges, and a noble
death in fight.*

Charles Kingsley,
The Heroes

*The death of Balder hastened the day of doom. Beauty and innocence were
gone from the earth. Violence and all the ways of evil increased.
Brother fought against brother, and son against father.*

*Sunlight and warmth grew less on the earth. There came three
years like one long winter, when bitter winds blew from every
quarter and snow piled in great drifts. The sun and the moon were
darkened in the heavens and the stars were quenched. . . .*

*Yet, as was told in the prophecies, this was not the end. After
darkness and silence, a new day came. Out of the sea arose a new
earth, green and fair, whose fields bore harvest without the sowing
of seed. A new sun, daughter of the old, shone in the heavens, even
more beautiful than her mother. All the ancient evil was passed and
gone. Balder was again among the living, and light and beauty returned to the earth.*

Dorothy Hosford,
Thunder of the Gods

GODS AND MEN

 Like the fairy tales, whose origins are lost in the origins of races, the myths have their source in the childhood of the race itself. Though they come to us out of so remote a past, the freshness and beauty, wonder and terror of these earliest stories of the world have still the power to enchant us as the tales unfold.

The word mythology comes from the Greek, and means "stories." And since the earliest Greek stories were about gods and men, we have come to associate myths with those stories in which primitive peoples, in their effort to understand the mystery of life and of natural phenomena, explained the world in which they found themselves.

A child of today asks "why" and "how" as he wonders about the natural world which he does not understand. So, in the childhood of the race, without knowledge of the discoveries with which science has enlarged our understanding, primitive peoples made their own explanations of the physical world in terms of themselves. They personified the natural forces. Thunder was the voice of Zeus to the Greeks, the hammer blows of Thor to the Norsemen. Primitive man peopled the world of nature with beings like himself, but invested with higher powers since natural forces were to him mysterious and beyond human control.

While each people invented its own explanations and turned them into stories, when these came to be written down, those of the Greeks have been found to exceed all others in beauty of imagination, in poetic conception, and in grace of expression. The chief sources of our knowledge of the Greek myths are found in the *Metamorphoses* of Ovid, a Roman poet, in the odes of the early Greek poets, especially in the odes of Pindar, and in the Greek dramatists, Sophocles and Euripides. There are also references to these stories in Homer and

Hesiod, and a prose collection was made by Apollodorus in the second century B.C.

Many of the myths, that were a part of the oral tradition of the Greeks, were never written down, or were lost. These have to be pieced together from several sources—from a flashing phrase of Greek poetry or a glancing reference in Greek drama, a reference which presupposes a common knowledge of stories as old as the race itself. Fragmentary as some of them are, they still after thousands of years cast the greatest spell of all in their poetry and imaginative power. To read them is to experience the wonder of the morning of the world; it is to see Artemis flashing through the cool green shade of the woods, or golden Aphrodite descending some hillside of many-fountained Ida, or the rainbow-winged Iris reflected in the sky as she brought the will of the gods to mortals. From the wood and water myths with their poetry, pathos, and grace comes, too, the story of the nymph Echo who lost her voice through the anger of Hera, and who could only watch in tears when the young Narcissus found death in the depths of the pool, not knowing it was his own fair face he had seen reflected in the waters of Helicon.

As well as the nature myths there are the stories of Perseus, Theseus, and the Argonauts, stories of heroic achievement filled with action and magic which tell of quests and of contests of skill, in which the gods give aid or wreak vengeance on mortals. The chief source of the story of the quest of the Golden Fleece is the *Argonautica* of Apollonius Rhodius, while the outlines of the tales of Perseus and Theseus are found in Apollodorus and in Plutarch. But when versions of these stories are made for children, the lack of specific detail in the available sources leaves a good deal of leeway for individual inter-pretation on the part of the reteller. It is more difficult to evaluate the different versions of the myths for children than the versions of the Iliad and the Odyssey, for instance, since there is no literary source for the myths comparable with Homer.

In comparing versions written for children, it is easily seen how widely interpretations may differ, particularly when we look at the same story as it is related, for instance, by Kingsley in *The Heroes*, by Hawthorne in *A Wonder-Book*, and, more recently, by Padraic Colum in *The Golden Fleece and the Heroes Who Lived before Achilles*.

Before looking at the retold stories themselves, let us first consider what we may expect to find in a version for children, or rather, what a writer should bring to the telling of these old tales. Too often the Greek myths have been retold for children by writers who saw in them only ready-made stories requiring no creative power on the part of the reteller, not realizing that unless the retelling recreates the spirit of the story as it is told in the original sources, the tale becomes lifeless and a mere relation of external events.

To recreate a story, there must first of all be a sympathy between the writer and the material he uses. Perhaps Charles Kingsley has best expressed this sympathy when he says in his introduction to *The Heroes* "Now, I love these old Hellens heartily." If a story is to hold interest for the reader it must first have engaged the interest and sympathy of the writer so that his feeling for the material is felt in the expression he gives to the story.

Before he begins to write, a reteller needs to absorb not the stories alone, but the whole environment of their setting. Only in this way can he feel at ease with his material and write from a knowledge of the life and thought of the people among whom the stories originated. This way of life, or point of view, has a national significance which distinguishes the myths of one country from those of any other and should be understood by the writer who interprets traditional literature.

The country from which the Greek myths sprang was a country of great natural beauty, of snow-capped mountains and wooded groves, of austere headlands and sunny seas. Here lived a race of men, creative and artistic, who early reached a maturity and a perfection in the arts acknowledged to be greater than has been attained by any race since. The stories they told are, as Hawthorne tells us, indestructible; they belong not only to the classic age of Greece but to every age, not alone through the pleasure they give as stories, but because so much great literature, in which allusions to the Greek myths abound, becomes unintelligible to the reader who has never heard them. The version in which they are read or heard becomes important when we realize the difference in the quality of the pleasure to be found in a good retelling as compared with one less good. The difference is still greater when we compare the wonder, poetry, and freshness of the original story with a version that is bald and matter-of-fact, stripped of any power to show us that early world whose beauty and magical influence grows brighter the more we know of its treasure store.

The versions which Kingsley, Hawthorne, and Colum have written for children appeal to us as literature in much the same sense as the best versions of the fairy tales are literature. The widely varied and personal interpretations of the three versions are the result of three quite different but entirely clear conceptions of what each writer meant to do with his material. This becomes evident as we study the manner in which each of the three writers approaches the subject and his personal relation to it.

Kingsley is completely in sympathy with the classic age of Greece. He viewed the Grecian gifts to posterity with a philosophy and a detachment which is brought out in his theme that man cannot prosper without the assistance of the gods. When Kingsley defines a hero as a man "who dares do more than other men" his explanation is given in the words of Athene to Perseus, "to the souls of fire I give more fire and to those who are manful I give a might more than man's . . . through doubt and need, danger and battle I drive them." When Perseus attempts the adventure of the Gorgon's head, it is with the sword and shield and sandals of the immortal gods that he leaps from the cliff into the empty air, "And behold, instead of falling he floated, and stood, and ran along the sky. He looked back, but Athene had vanished, and Hermes; and the sandals led him on northward ever, like a crane who follows the spring toward the Ister fens."

Kingsley's version keeps that sense of wonder inherent in the unsophisticated era of Greek thought. He is able to give, too, a sense of the widening world beyond their own shores, of which the Greeks heard perhaps from tales told by venturesome travelers. In search of the Grey Sisters, Kingsley tells us, Perseus "came to the edge of the everlasting night, where the air was full of feathers, and the soil was hard with ice; and there he found the three Grey Sisters by the shore of the freezing sea." And later, after the slaying of the Gorgon, Perseus sees on his homeward way "the long green garden of Egypt and the shining stream of Nile."

Kingsley brings out, in his telling, the quality of cold justice meted out in Greek literature to evil men. The scene when Perseus returns to the palace of King Polydectes, as Kingsley describes it, has the drama of a Greek play:

> "Those whom the Gods help fulfil their promises: and those who despise them, reap as they have sown. Behold the Gorgon's head!" Then Perseus drew back the goat-skin, and held aloft the Gorgon's head.
>
> Pale grew Polydectes and his guests as they looked upon that dreadful face. They tried to rise up from their seats: but from

their seats they never rose, but stiffened, each man where he sat, into a ring of cold grey stones.

The simple dignity of the telling, the pure choice of words, the music and rhythm of Kingsley's language, give a sense of "rightness" for stories which were in the first place meant to be listened to, and which were also in some form of poetry.

When we turn to Hawthorne's version of the story, we seem to be in a different world from that of Kingsley's *Heroes,* as indeed we are. For while both tell essentially the same story, Hawthorne's intention is very different from Kingsley's. The difficulty of comparison lies in Hawthorne's personal interpretation which is so much his own and so far removed from the conception of classic Greece as to be almost an individual creation.

The story of "The Gorgon's Head" in *The Wonder Book* is more a fairy tale than a tale of the gods. But this was Hawthorne's clear intention. In his hands the story has assumed, as he himself tells us, "a Gothic or romantic guise." He describes Perseus as the hero of a fairy tale might be pictured; he is "a handsome youth, very strong and active, and skilful in the use of arms." The gods are friendly and mischievous playfellows with gifts of magic. Their speech is the everyday speech of men, and they make no claim to such unlimited power as Athene has in Kingsley's version. Instead, Quicksilver tells Perseus that "I am the very person to help you, if anybody can." Later, Quicksilver remarks, "I generally have all my wits about me, such as they are." This fairy tale aspect is seen also in the excellent names given to the three Grey Sisters: "Scarecrow," "Nightmare," and "Shakejoint." The familiar use of three is carried on in the three gifts of the nymphs to Perseus—the flying slippers, the magic wallet, and the helmet of darkness.

In Hawthorne's version we see the free and happy play of his intellect finding expression in quick and lively narration. He writes simply and spontaneously, embroidering his tale with obvious delight in his own inventive fancy. Although his occasional tongue-in-cheek comments interrupt the story, it still retains an ingenuous quality of pure pleasure in the telling of the story for its own sake.

Padraic Colum's version uses a form of the story of "The Gorgon's Head" different from that of either Kingsley or Hawthorne.[1] His version is shorter, of necessity, since it is introduced as one of the stories

[1] Padraic Colum, *The Golden Fleece and the Heroes Who Lived before Achilles* (N.Y.: Macmillan, 1921).

which Orpheus sang to the heroes who went in search of the Golden
Fleece. Because of this method of construction the story seems to
lack the stature of the other two versions, but this does not diminish
Colum's virtuosity as a teller of marvelous tales.

The technique he uses in his version is one with which readers of
his books are familiar. He begins the story in the middle with Perseus'
appearance at the cave of the Grey Sisters, goes back to the beginning,
and from thence on to the end. This is Colum's device to allow Perseus
to tell his own account of his adventures to the nymphs who give
him the magic gifts which enable him to slay the Gorgon. Homer uses
a similar method in allowing Odysseus to relate in his own words his
earlier adventures before he is cast ashore at Phaeacia. In this way
Colum is able to give a certain raciness and vivacity to the personal
narrative of Perseus. At the same time the adventures are compressed
into as brief a space as possible.

Padraic Colum is at ease with fantasy and is sensitive to the wonder
of the Greek stories. He conveys this wonder by his use of language
and his selection of incidents; he makes the stories more than fairy
tales, yet they are not stories of the gods in the sense that Kingsley's
are. In his conception of the Greek myths, Colum stands somewhere
between Kingsley and Hawthorne. Kingsley deals with the gods in
the tradition of Homer. They appear and disappear at needed times,
sometimes in person, sometimes as visions, but always they have, in
our minds, the dignity of their high position in relation to mortals.
Belief in their power is conveyed in Kingsley's version of the stories.
Hawthorne, on the other hand, looks on the gods with casual disbelief.
In his telling of the stories he seems to be saying, "You are not simple
enough to think that the meaning of them is true, and true forever."

Hawthorne's conception of the Greek myths is, in his own words,
that of "capital" stories, capable of being "shaped anew as his fancy
dictated." His fancy is of a high order and makes diverting reading of
these old stories which he embroiders with delicacy and charm.
Kingsley on the other hand has a classic conception of the Greek
myths. He has filled them with light and sunshine and blue skies, and
with the beauty, wonder, and agelessness of that early world. Hawthorne and Kingsley represent two points of view, two intentions,
both of which have added treasure to literature for children, but it
is undeniable that the classic conception of Kingsley's *Heroes* is
truer to the heroic age of Greece.

At first glance, the Norse myths may seem bare, terse, even unpoetic in comparison with the myths of the Greeks. The universe on which All-Father Odin looked out from his lofty watchtower is a different world from the one ruled by Zeus, for the myths of each race, as they try to interpret the natural world, reflect their own natural surroundings. To the Greeks, nature was for the most part soft and kind. They lived under blue skies, their landscape bright with color and sunshine. To the Norsemen, nature was more often an enemy. Ice, snow, frost, and blustering winds made their landscape of rocks and boulders, rushing rivers and dark valleys, majestic and awe-inspiring. So the stark dramatic simplicity of the telling of the Norse myths reflects inevitably the stern northern scene.

Unlike the Greek myths, which, when they came to be written down, were still the belief of those who related them, the Norse myths were compiled when Iceland had been a Christian country for over a hundred years. *The Prose Edda* by a twelfth century Icelandic writer, Snorri the priest, is an important source of our knowledge of Norse mythology. While Snorri no longer believed in the old Norse gods, he believed in the imaginative truth of these tales from his country's remotest past, seeing in them the greatness and nobility of its traditional oral literature.

To the Icelanders, their literature, prose sagas and poetry, was an important and necessary part of their national culture. Snorri compiled his *Prose Edda* as a handbook for young poets. The stories he tells there are not told as a mere compilation of the events and details of the myths as he knew them. *The Prose Edda* is more than a source book, for it goes back to the earliest narratives of the Old Norse, and gives life to a literature which reflects the ideas, the moral development, and the actual customs and habits of the childhood of their race.

Consider how much homely detail there is in Norse mythology; detail which reveals that in a bleak, northern country the Norseman preserved his life at the cost of individual effort and resource under austere circumstances. Before Hermod tries to leap over the gate of Hel, we see him dismount from his horse, Sleipnir, to tighten the girths and make all secure. Yet Hermod was a god and Sleipnir no mortal horse. When Hermod has leaped over the gate, he walks into Hel's hall and sees there in the high seat "Balder, his brother." Balder sends a ring to his father Odin "for a remembrance" and his wife "a linen smock" to Frigg. The homely detail adds to the humor in some of the stories and gives pathos to others, but in each and all it gives effectiveness to the picture of the simple way of life of these early Norsemen.

The form of the Norse myths differs from the Greek to as great an extent as their content and ideas. The Norse stories are compressed, terse, and dramatic. There is very little narrative or description, and much direct speech. A great deal is taken for granted in the individual stories which can only be known by reference to the others. For instance, in the story of the death of Balder we are told little of Balder himself. It is assumed that the reader would know of Balder, as we ourselves would know of King Arthur or Joan of Arc. The allusions to Balder in other stories tell us more by implication than by actual statements, but what we read of him persuades us that the death of Balder was surely "the greatest mischance that has ever befallen among gods and men."

The literary convention of the original Norse poetry is not rhyme but alliteration. The verses are simply constructed and easily translated into alliterative English verse. Unlike Greek poetry which abounds in long, involved metaphors, the Norse has none. Instead, we find a device called a "kenning" by which, in periphrasis, something, or someone, is referred to, not by name, but by a term which is understood only through a knowledge of the story which explains it. For instance, gold is called "Sif's hair," Sigurd is "Fafnir's bane."

Kennings are not used to any extent in the mythological poems. Their greater use in skaldic poetry resulted from the lack of metaphor and other poetic devices in Norse poetry. The strength and beauty of the mythological poems is in their imaginative and dramatic force, not in their embroidery or adornment, which is negligible.

The Norse myths have an ever-present undertone of tragedy. While the gods of the Greeks are always young and know themselves to be immortal, the Norse gods have foreknowledge of their eventual destruction. This note of unpreventable disaster recurs throughout the stories, giving them a tragic yet heroic undertone not found in any other mythology. In the story of "The Apples of Iduna" we are told "she guards in her chest of ash those apples which the gods must taste whensoever they grow old; and then they all become young, and so it shall be even unto the Weird of the Gods." The gods know their end is foreordained but they do not for that reason cease their resistance against the giants and all evil forces that are the enemies of men. In the last dreadful battle the gods must be overthrown, but in defeat they become even more heroic, fighting bravely against hopeless odds.

In one of the older poems of *The Poetic Edda*, "Voluspo," there is given a picture of the new fair world that will rise from the ashes of the old. Its promise lightens the sombre gloom of the "Weird of the Gods."

> Now do I see the earth anew
> Rise all green from the waves again;
> The cataracts fall and the eagle flies
> And fish he catches beneath the cliffs.
>
> In wondrous beauty once again
> Shall the golden tables stand mid the grass,
> Which the gods had owned in the days of old,
> Then fields unsowed bear ripened fruit,
> All ills grow better and Baldr comes back.

To retell for children the stories of Norse mythology presents one difficulty common to both the Norse and the Greek myths. They are condensed, often fragmentary, or obscure. But beyond this, all resemblance ceases. The power of the Norse myths is dramatic rather than narrative or descriptive and so is more akin to the simple, terse folk tale in its swift-moving account of dramatic events.

A reteller may try to re-create the stories by expanding them where they are condensed, adding his own details and explanations where they are fragmentary and obscure, and his own ornamentation and embroidery where they are bare. To do this without destroying the whole feeling and significance of the myths is difficult to achieve. For instance A. and E. Keary's version of "Iduna's Apples" in *The Heroes of Asgard*, with its expanded descriptions of the grove and of Iduna, befits an elaborate fairy tale.

> It was a still, bright evening. The leaves of the trees moved softly up and down, whispering sweet words to each other; the flowers, with half-shut eyes, nodded sleepily to their own reflections in the water, and Iduna sat by the fountain, with her head resting in one hand, thinking of pleasant things.
>
> Iduna, the mistress of the grove, was fit to live among young birds, and tender leaves, and spring flowers. She was so fair that when she bent over the river to entice her swans to come to her, even the stupid fish stood still in the water, afraid to destroy so beautiful an image by swimming over it; and when she held out her

hand with bread for the swans to eat, you would not have known it from a water-lily—it was so wonderfully white.

Although their attempt to "prettify" the Norse myths loses the feeling and significance of the original stories, there are, at times, descriptive phrases such as "the wide-glancing most sunlit of palaces" (Balder's) which show an imaginative conception in sympathy with the stories they use. Again, in their version of Balder's death we find "Hodur threw—Balder fell, and the shadow of death covered the whole earth," lines which in spite of the affected style are as tersely and dramatically expressed as the Eddas. But on the whole, while the Keary version has high moments of imaginative understanding, the invented detail and manner of telling is unlike the spirit of the Norse myths and not representative of their style, which is graphic and terse rather than descriptive and amplified.

Abbie Farwell Brown has approached the retelling of the Norse myths with a different intention. *In the Days of Giants* follows the original stories more closely than *The Heroes of Asgard,* and tries to recreate them in the bare, simple manner of the Eddas. Here, for instance, is the opening paragraph of "How Odin Lost His Eye":

> In the beginning of things, before there was any world or sun, moon, and stars, there were the giants; for these were the oldest creatures that ever breathed. They lived in Jotunheim, the land of frost and darkness, and their hearts were evil. Next came the gods, the good Aesir, who made earth and sky and sea, and who dwelt in Asgard, above the heavens. Then were created the queer little dwarfs, who lived underground in the caverns of the mountains, working at their mines of metal and precious stones. Last of all, the gods made men to dwell in Midgard, the good world that we know, between which and the glorious home of the Aesir stretched Bifrost, the bridge of rainbows.

This is forceful, clear, and terse, although the effect is somewhat weakened by the reference to the "queer little dwarfs." But while Abbie Farwell Brown does not attempt to add the imaginative embroideries we find in the Keary version of the Norse myths, she was influenced by the moral and didactic ideas of her time. She tells the stories simply, but imparts to the telling a moral tone, inserting phrases such as "which is always the way of evil-doers." She adds, as well, much explanatory detail which gives her telling a general air of condescension. The "iron bands" with which the gods bound Loki in punishment for the death of Balder are explained as "Loki's evil passions." The "ugly toads, snakes and insects" which inhabit the cave where Loki is imprisoned are "Loki's evil thoughts, who were to live with him henceforth and torment him always." By reducing the stories to the plane of everyday moralizing, Abbie Farwell Brown loses much of the significance, moral and literary, of mythology as such. The myths contain moral ideas of right and wrong, good and evil, as they also interpret the phenomena of life or nature, but their explanation and interpretation is implicit and is better left to the perception and imagination of the reader or listener.

There is another way of retelling the Norse myths for children, a way that retains the brief, direct, dramatic nature of the original stories, taking advantage at the same time of all the available imaginative detail so as to bring out in its full force each dramatic incident and situation. This way of recreating the Norse myths makes great demands on the reteller. It asks for more than a surface familiarity with the events of the stories. The reteller must also understand the world of ideas in the Eddas, their vast conception of the creation of the world and its ultimate destruction, their powerful and dramatic atmosphere which is alive with tremendous events.

This way of telling the Norse myths is found in Dorothy Hosford's *Thunder of the Gods*. She tells them in the direct and simple fashion characteristic of the Eddas and also of the Norse folk tales. At the same time she has done the "sorting out" of the material which is necessary to keep the stories uncomplicated and unconfused. Here, for instance, is her description of Balder in the story which tells of his death:

> Balder was the fairest and most beloved of the gods. He was wise in judgment, gracious in speech, and all his deeds were pure and good. Wherever Balder went there was joy and warmth and gladness. He was beloved by gods and men, and so beautiful that the whitest flower which grew on the hillside was named "Balder's Brow."[2]

In the original story, as Snorri tells it, the reader's familiarity with Balder is taken for granted since Snorri wrote in a time when the stories of the gods were common knowledge. Dorothy Hosford's introduction to the story contains not only the implication of everything that

[2] Dorothy Hosford, *Thunder of the Gods* (N.Y.: Holt, 1952). This and the quotations on pages 76 and 78 are used by permission.

is told of Balder in the Eddas, but expresses, as well, the Norse ideal of god-like qualities. Without this knowledge the reader or listener must fail to realize the full import of the tragedy of Balder's death.

Although the stories in *Thunder of the Gods* are told in the simple, terse, direct manner of the folk tale, they are also told in a heightened language which recreates the dramatic form of the original stories. For instance, after the introduction quoted above, Dorothy Hosford begins her story of the death of Balder with his dreams, which is its real beginning:

> It came about that Balder dreamed great and perilous dreams concerning his life. Night after night they troubled his sleep. When Balder spoke of these dreams to the other gods they were filled with foreboding. They knew that some danger threatened him and all the gods took council together as to how they might save Balder.

In order to appraise the force and beauty of these few, simple sentences let us compare them with Abbie Farwell Brown's account of Balder and the Mistletoe. She begins the story with a long paragraph about Loki, attributing to him many imagined-by-herself feelings and motives of revenge, until "whenever in the dark he passed unseen, the gods shuddered as if a breath of evil had blown upon them, and even the flowers drooped before his steps." This is followed by her version of Balder's dreams:

> Now at this time Balder the beautiful had a strange dream. He dreamed that a cloud came before the sun, and all Asgard was dark. He waited for the cloud to drift away, and for the sun to smile again. But no; the sun was gone forever, he thought; and Balder awoke feeling very sad. The next night Balder had another dream. This time he dreamed that it was still dark as before; the flowers were withered and the gods were growing old; even Idun's magic apples could not make them young again. And all were weeping and wringing their hands as though some dreadful thing had happened. Balder awoke feeling strangely frightened, yet he said no word to Nanna his wife, for he did not want to trouble her.
>
> When it came night again Balder slept and dreamed a third dream, a still more terrible one than the other two had been. He thought that in the dark, lonely world there was nothing but a sad voice, which cried, "The sun is gone! The spring is gone! Joy is gone! For Balder the beautiful is dead, dead, dead!"[3]

[3] Abbie Farwell Brown, *In the Days of Giants* (Boston: Houghton, Mifflin, 1902), p.11.

Following the disclosure of Balder's dream, his wife "ran sobbing" to Frigg. Frigg "was frightened almost out of her wits" and exclaims "I will travel all over the world and make all things promise not to injure my boy." This invented detail and everyday vernacular is so unlike the spirit of the Eddas that even the dramatic moments lose conviction.

The death of Balder is the climax of the stories of the gods told in Norse mythology. It is related by Snorri with moving simplicity and pathos.

> Then, when Baldr was fallen, words failed all the Aesir, and their hands likewise to lay hold of him; each looked at the other, and all were of one mind as to who had wrought the work, yet none might take vengeance, so great a sanctuary was in that place. But when the Aesir tried to speak, then it befell first that weeping broke out, so that none might speak to the others with words concerning his grief. But Odin bore that misfortune by so much the worst, that he had most perception of how great harm and loss for the Aesir were in the death of Baldr.

Abbie Farwell Brown's version is as follows:

> Oh, the sad thing that befell! Straight through the air flew the little arrow, straight as magic and Loki's arm could direct it. Straight to Balder's heart it sped, piercing through jerkin and shirt and all, to give its bitter message of "Loki's love," as he had said. With a cry Balder fell forward on the grass. And that was the end of sunshine and spring and joy in Asgard, for the dream had come true, and Balder the beautiful was dead.
>
> When the Aesir saw what had happened, there was a great shout of fear and horror, and they rushed upon Hod, who had thrown the fatal arrow.
>
> "What is it? What have I done?" asked the poor blind brother, trembling at the tumult which had followed his shot.
>
> "You have slain Balder!" cried the Aesir. "Wretched Hod, how could you do it?"
>
> "It was the old woman—the evil old woman, who stood at my elbow and gave me a little twig to throw," gasped Hod. "She must be a witch."
>
> Then the Aesir scattered over Ida Plain to look for the old woman who had done the evil deed; but she had mysteriously disappeared.
>
> "It must be Loki," said wise Heimdal, "It is Loki's last and vilest trick."

"Oh, my Balder, my beautiful Balder!" wailed Queen Frigg, throwing herself on the body of her son. "If I had only made the mistletoe give me the promise, you would have been saved. It was I who told Loki of the mistletoe,—so it is I who have killed you. Oh, my son, my son!"

Abbie Farwell Brown loses sight of the understatement of the original which gives it force and pathos. Instead she brings it down to the plane of melodrama. If we contrast this with Dorothy Hosford's telling of Balder's death, we are at once aware of the difference between a version written out of a knowledge of the inner significance of the story, and one without it.

Hod took the mistletoe wand and shot at Balder, and Loki guided his hand.

The shaft flew through Balder and he fell dead to the earth. This was the greatest mischance that has ever befallen gods and men.

When Balder fell to the earth the gods could not speak a word for grief and anguish, nor could they move to lift him where he lay. Each looked at the other and they were all of one mind whose evil hand had done this deed. Yet they could take no revenge for they stood on hallowed ground.

When they tried to speak the tears came and the gods wept bitterly for the loss of Balder. They had no words with which to name their sorrow. Of them all Odin grieved most, for he understood best how great was the loss which had come to the gods.

The mother of Balder was the first to speak. "If any among you," said Frigg, "would win all my love and favor, let him ride the road to Hel and seek Balder among the dead. Let him offer Hel a ransom if she will but let Balder come home to Asgard."

This almost stark directness of telling is in keeping with the original and gives a sense of remoteness and dignity befitting a story of the gods.

In *Thunder of the Gods*, Dorothy Hosford tells the Norse myths with strength, clarity, and cohesion. She is able to achieve dramatic effect through her terse, swift narration of events, not described, but expressed in action. She recreates the original stories through forceful conversation within the narrative which crystallizes the persons of the story and brings out both the comic and tragic interplay of ambitions, fears, longings, and despair. There is a spaciousness of atmosphere in her use of language which conveys to the reader or listener the unforgettable impress of its valid poetic quality. *Thunder of the Gods* recreates for children the Norse myths of the Eddas as Charles Kingsley with similar respect, affection, and distinction has given children the Greek myths in his book *The Heroes.*

ASSOCIATIVE READING

DAWSON, WARREN ROYAL. The Bridle of Pegasus; Studies in Magic, Mythology and Folklore. Methuen, 1930.

KOHT, HALVDAN. The Old Norse Sagas. American Scandinavian Foundation, 1945.

MUNCH, PETER ANDREAS. Norse Mythology; Legends of Gods and Heroes, tr. from the Norwegian by Sigurd Bernhard Hustvedt. American Scandinavian Foundation, 1926.

PHILLPOTTS, BERTHA S. Edda and Saga. Holt, 1932. Thornton Butterworth, 1931. (Home University Library)

STURLUSON, SNORRI. The Prose Edda, tr. from the Icelandic with an introd. by Arthur Gilchrist Brodeue. American Scandinavian Foundation, 1929.

CHAPTER SIX

Now vainly mortal men do blame the gods. For of us they say comes evil, whereas they even of themselves, through the blindness of their own hearts, have sorrows beyond that which is ordained.

The Odyssey

Ye have heard of Sigurd aforetime, how the foes of God he slew;
How forth from the darksome desert the Gold of the Waters he drew;
How he wakened Love on the mountain, and wakened Brynhild the Bright,
And dwelt upon earth for a season, and shone in all men's sight.

William Morris,
The Story of Sigurd the Volsung

This is the great story of the north, which should be to our race what the Tale of Troy was to the Greeks—to all our race first, and afterwards, when the change of the world has made our race nothing more than a name of what has been—a story too—then should it be to those who come after us no less than the Tale of Troy has been to us.

William Morris,
The Story of the Volsungs and Niblungs

HEROES OF EPIC AND SAGA

What is an epic? In what way does it differ from other traditional literature such as folk tales and myths? What is its value and use today? Does it still give pleasure to the reader or listener? These are some of the questions we ponder as we consider the versions for children of these stories from the heroic age.

The heroic age of any nation is one in which the ideals of the nation take form in the character and actions of the great heroes who embody the national ideals. Their heroic deeds are sung by minstrels at the halls and hearths of the people, stirring their national pride and giving stature to the tradition of the people from whom their heroes sprung.

These stories of heroes sung by minstrels were often scattered and fragmentary, and would so remain unless it should happen that the creative genius of a poet saw in this material a story he wished to tell. For an epic poem tells a story which, while it deals with legendary matter, is built into a noble structure of solid significance. It is from the greatness of the poet's conception that the poem gains its significance, both for its own time, and for us who read it in this present day.

We today are not part of the process of growth of traditional literature. In the epic we approach traditional material in a literary and artistic form—a form which is an integral part of its quality and which has contributed to its survival. If we are to apply a standard of judgment in evaluating versions for children of the epics of any country, our understanding of the significance, as well as the content and style of the original epic, must inform our judgment before we can know whether a translator or reteller has handled the material with respect, integrity, and imaginative insight.

Few of us have a knowledge of Greek, and so our understanding of the greatest of all epic poems, Homer's *Iliad* and *Odyssey,* is gained through translations. Here again our inability to read the original poem makes it necessary for us to accept the word of scholars in regard to the translation that is closest to the conception of the original.

To read *The Odyssey,* for instance, in either the Butcher and Lang or the Palmer translation, both of which have been praised by scholars, is to experience the excitement of superb storytelling, for *The Odyssey* is one of the greatest stories in the world. We are caught up in the sweep of the action and the beauty of the language. We are moved by the emotions which move the characters in the story and are filled with concern and anxiety for their difficulties. As we read, some recognition of the Homeric world illumines our minds. We know its early dawn and its wine-dark seas, the black ships cutting the waves with the rowers sitting "well in order"; we know the rocky shores and headlands; the tilled fields and crops, the goats and cattle which were of so great concern to the kings as well as to the herdsmen. We know the kings' houses and the huts of the simple shepherds, what each one ate and drank and wore and in what fashion he passed his days. And we know the men and the women themselves, what things they held dear and what was matter for scorn. In spite of aspects of violence theirs was a spacious life in which they moved with simple dignity. They valued reverence toward the gods, loyalty to one's friends, welcome and graciousness toward the stranger, retribution for injury, and above all a steadfast courage in the face of whatever doom the gods might send.

The construction or pattern of *The Odyssey* is in three parts. Homer shows us first of all the misrule of Ithaca, the kingdom of Odysseus, by the suitors of Penelope; the helplessness of both Penelope and Telemachus to prevent the suitors from despoiling the kingdom because of their numbers and strength. In despair Telemachus leaves Ithaca to find news of his father Odysseus. The suitors, finding him gone, plot the death of Telemachus on his return journey.

The second part is an account of the adventures of Odysseus, who is balked by cruel fate at every turn in his purpose to return to Ithaca after the war with Troy. The narrative carries the story from Odysseus' imprisonment on Calypso's isle to his arrival at the palace of Alcinous, King of Phaeacia. Here Odysseus gives the king his own account of his adventures, and so the adventures from the fall of Troy to the shores of Phaeacia are related as a personal narrative.

By this device the narrative gains speed and urgency, becomes graphic and dramatic, since only the events which are of importance to Odysseus are related by him. The character of Odysseus becomes clear to us through his own words and actions. We see him resolute in purpose, far-seeing, and resourceful ("Odysseus of many devices"), outwitting fate and enemy, loving deeply his own land and home, and unswerving in courage where others would have despaired of ever winning home in the face of such odds.

The third part of the story puts Odysseus ashore on his own island of Ithaca where he learns of the state of his kingdom in the power of the suitors. Odysseus assumes the disguise of a beggar in order to carry out his plan of vengeance on the suitors and so regain his kingdom. He is joined by the safely-returned Telemachus and the stage is set for the final act—the rout of the suitors and the reunion with Penelope.

All three parts are really stories within the story. We are aware of the noble design, of the unity of Homer's artistic purpose, and of a poetic expression equal to a theme of profound and universal significance. *The Odyssey* is a tale of action, yet beyond the outward incidents it has a national significance which relates it inevitably to the well-ordered aesthetic civilization of Greece. *The Odyssey* is an expression of the temper of mind, way of thought, of a national culture which has put the whole civilized world in its debt.

Through the story as Homer tells it, the *humanness* of Greek life is felt in the details of living. The pursuits, even of those of noble birth, are close to the earth. The kings show concern for their flocks and fields, the queens for the daily affairs of their households. We feel too the importance of the roles played by people of humble birth, the swineherd, the old nurse, and we are touched by the simple dignity with which they are presented. Above all we feel their human affection, grief, loss, joy, pride, despair. In an epic we find the events of commonplace life told from the point of view of an ideal man of the race; this point of view, embodying as it does the ideals of the race, gives greater dignity to the expression of the story.

Any version of *The Odyssey* for boys and girls should carry the reader on through the story with the swiftness and urgency that is in Homer's poem. It should convey the ideals, the temper of mind of the people whose heroic tradition is sung by the poet. And since *The Odyssey* is Greek narrative poetry at its greatest, a version of the story should convey something of the heightened language of Homer's poetry which has immortalized the story he told.

The unreluctant years

The story of Odysseus has been told and retold for children by a number of writers from the time of Charles Lamb up to the present day. Some of these versions lack any resemblance to Homer's poem except in giving an outline of the events of the story. The best versions attempt to convey the dignity of Greek epic poetry and the classic feeling for the need of noble words to express noble deeds.

When Charles Lamb told the story of *The Adventures of Ulysses,* his source was Chapman, not Homer's poem, which he had never read. Lamb's version is in harmony with Chapman in that it has at times the ornamentation and extravagant fancy of Elizabethan poetry, but it has as well many truly poetic phrases from Homer that are found in Chapman's translation. *The Adventures of Ulysses* is not free from archaisms; at times it is so concise and condensed that we miss the detail of dress and houses, food, and manners which in Homer add to the sense of reality and to the pictorial value of the story. But Charles Lamb's way of telling *The Adventures of Ulysses,* with its dramatic feeling, dignity of style, balanced sentences, elaborate metaphors, and Greek epithets, is still the only version of *The Odyssey* for children which has literary value apart from its identity as a retelling. Other versions have given perhaps a more faithful transcript of the original, but they have not given us new classics such as Kingsley and Hawthorne made of the Greek myths.

In evaluating versions of *The Odyssey* for children, we have a single source, Homer. But since a knowledge of the original poem is inaccessible except to classical scholars, our best secondary source is found in the translations into English whose fidelity to the original is acknowledged. From our reading of the Butcher and Lang and the Palmer translations, we can observe, in versions of *The Odyssey* for children, differences in the handling of the main outline; in the detail included, and in the quality of expression each reteller is able to give to the story he tells.

The Odyssey for Boys and Girls, by Alfred J. Church, is a simple account which begins with the adventure on the island of the Cyclops and follows the return journey as far as the island of Calypso. At this point, Church leaves Odysseus and takes us to Ithaca, telling the story of the suitors of Penelope and of the journey of Telemachus in search of news of his father. The story then returns to Calypso's isle, carries Odysseus at last back to Ithaca, and ends with the slaying of the suitors. The interpolation of the story of Telemachus in the middle of the adventures of Odysseus, slows the dramatic swiftness of events and breaks the unity of Homer's plan of *The Odyssey*. It is true, however, that the adventure with the Cyclops provides an arresting opening for the story which arouses the immediate interest of children in the further adventures of Odysseus.

Colum's *Children's Homer* follows at first the sequence of events as Homer tells them, but instead of having Telemachus return to Ithaca on learning of his father's captivity on Calypso's island, Colum holds him in Sparta to hear the whole story of the Trojan war as told in Homer's *Iliad*.

In part two of his story, Colum tells of Odysseus' escape from Calypso and of his coming to Phaeacia where he relates his adventures to the king and is given aid to return to Ithaca. Then follows the slaying of the suitors and the story ends. There is something to be said for having the story of *The Iliad* and *The Odyssey* in one account, and Colum's way of handling the matter still preserves the unity of both *The Iliad* and *The Odyssey*.

The simplicity and directness of Church's version is gained by leaving out the long metaphors, much of the repetition, and all those passages which do not bear directly upon the main action. His style, though not distinguished, is plain and good. Colum has a greater resemblance to the style of the original but his writing is uneven. At times it is dignified and forceful, at other times casual and colloquial. Both ways of writing can be found on a single page. While *The Odyssey for Boys and Girls* and *The Children's Homer* are widely read and enjoyed, I feel that "the winged words" of Homer's *Odyssey* have yet to inspire some future writer before we will have a children's classic written in memorable language—one that will please the ear as well as the imagination, for this is a story which had its origin in Greek poetry and was intended to be listened to rather than read.

The simplicity, directness, and down-to-earth quality of Homer's epics have much in common with the sagas of the Norsemen. Reading *The Odyssey* or the *Grettis Saga*, for instance, stirs the same sense of inner excitement in response to their heroic themes, to the rapid movement of the narrative, and to the sheer drama of the human material they contain.

The word saga means simply things said or told; that is, the sagas began as an oral tradition, an exiled people remembering their past. Tales of their exploits, told in the long winter evenings about log fires, grew into an art of storytelling which, when the stories came to be written down, have given the Icelandic sagas a unique place in creative literature. Like the Greek epics, the sagas are swift, direct, and dramatic; they are unlike Homer in that they are written in prose narrative, not in the form of epic poetry, and they are for the most part anonymous.

The Icelandic sagas are less familiar to us than *The Iliad* and *The Odyssey* of Homer for the reason that, until comparatively recent years, translations into English have been lacking. Yet the language of the Icelanders, more than others, is akin to our own; and while the Greek epics have come down to us as a part of world literature, the Icelandic sagas belong to our racial inheritance. They tell us how our forefathers lived, of their way of thinking, the laws they regarded, and the ideals they upheld.

The translations of the sagas most widely known are those by Sir George Dasent and William Morris. Since they did not both translate the same sagas and since the style of different sagas varies, a comparison is difficult. From both translators, however, the sagas emerge as literature. In his preface to his translation of Njal's saga, *Njála,* Dasent writes:

> Even now, after all that has been done to make the rendering faithful, the translator lays it with dread before the public, not because he has any doubt as to the beauty of his original, but because he is in despair, lest any shortcoming of his own should mar the noble features of the masterpiece which it has been his care to copy.

Dasent translates the sagas into simple, natural English, keeping as close to the wording of the original as possible. William Morris, on the other hand, with his greater feeling for the music and rhythm of language is less literal, less simple. He gives a smoother rendering which has the accent of dignity and heroic temper which we miss, to some extent, in Dasent, and which the originals undoubtedly possess. The occasional archaisms in the Morris translations are a stumbling block to the modern reader and obscure a version which otherwise is vivid and alive.

The "saga men" of Iceland—"that hard and lonely island in the high Atlantic"—were the storytellers of their communities and developed great narrative skill. The storyteller had to hold his listeners' attention night after night and so learned a way of telling a story simply, objectively, and in proportion, and at the same time with great dramatic

86

force. The speech of the Icelanders was the plain, practical, reserved speech of landowners and farmers, the expression of a people whose gift for language approaches the art of drama; that is, the interest depends on the power and truth of the dramatic situations and on the characters themselves as we see them in direct speech and action. For example, in the saga of Burnt Njal, when Gunnar is beset by his enemies he defends himself with his bow, but at last his bow-string is cut. He asks his wife for two strands of her long hair with which to make a new bow-string. "Is that worth much to you?" she asks. "My life depends on it," he answers; "so long as I have my bow I can hold my enemies off." "Then," she replies, "I shall remember that once you gave me a box on the ear, and I care not whether you defend yourself a longer or a shorter time." "Everybody wins fame in his own way," Gunnar retorts, and he fights until he can fight no more.

The two characters of Gunnar and his wife are here clearly opposed and revealed. In a few skilful lines of dramatic conversation the characters are made known to us. Their motives are recognized. The characteristic restraint of their speech gives vivid life to the far-off scene. This psychological interest in character-revealing conversation and action gives the sagas a modern interest. More than the heroes of epic poetry and medieval romance, the characters of the sagas are like men and women we can know and understand.

The sagas have a historical interest because they tell of the people who actually lived in Iceland between the ninth and the eleventh centuries, although the sagas themselves were not written down until the thirteenth century. Considering the sagas as a whole we can see, as in a tapestry, the recurring pattern in which the hero of one saga becomes a subordinate character in another, while a minor figure of the first now takes the leading part in a new saga. The men and women of the sagas were, in a sense, neighbors, and well known to one another, at least by reputation. Their paths cross and recross in different sagas. There is an instance in the *Grettis Saga* in which Grettir, an outlaw, takes shelter with Thorgils who also has as his guests Thorgeir and Thormod, the chief characters of the *Foster Brothers Saga*. The outcome of this association of three high-spirited men is discussed between Thorgils and Skapti:

> "It is true, Thorgils, that you have entertained those three men this winter, that are held to be the most regardless and overbearing, and all of them outlaws, and you have handled them so that none

has hurt another?" Yes, it was true, said Thorgils. Skapti said: "That is something for a man to be proud of; but what do you think of the three, and how are they each of them in courage?" Thorgils said: "They are all three bold men to the full; yet two of them, I think, may tell what fear is like. It is not in the same way with both; for Thormod fears God, and Grettir is so afraid of the dark that after dark he would never stir, if he had his own way; but I do not know that Thorgeir, my kinsman, is afraid of anything." "You have read them well," says Skapti; and so their talk ended.

This episode illustrates not only the reappearance of already familiar characters in a new saga; it brings to our notice, too, the interest in character which predominates in the sagas.

Each saga tells a story, usually the story of one generation of the family of an Icelandic landowner who is chief of his community. The human material of the story is of first importance—the characters, their actions and inter-actions, and the destined course their lives must take as a result. The technique of the saga is to reveal the causes of the action by letting us see things as they happen and draw our own conclusions. In the saga of Burnt Njal, Gunnar, under decree of banishment, sets out with Kolskegg for his ship. When they have gone a little way Gunnar's horse trips and throws him off. Then, looking back toward the Lithe and the homestead Gunnar says, "Fair is the Lithe; so fair that it has never seemed to me so fair; the corn fields are white to harvest, and the home mead is mown; and now I will ride back home, and not fare abroad at all."

No interpretation is given by the narrator for Gunnar's reason for deciding to return to his home, thereby courting death at the hands of his enemies. What is told by the storyteller is only what might have been seen and heard by any bystander. It is the march of events which relates cause and effect as the story moves swiftly and logically from incident to incident, preparing the listener for the ultimate tragedy, whether it is the burning of Njal in his house, or the slaying of Grettir in his lonely island retreat, or the humiliation of the last years of Egil, blind and feeble, ordered away by the kitchen maids from his seat by the hearth fire. It is in the unerring skill of the saga storyteller in choosing the revealing incident, that the pattern of the story grows, takes on significance, and is given unity.

The sagas vary in interest and in length, but in outline they are similar. Most of them follow the form of historical or biographical accounts of the times and persons of which they tell. But in the dramatic, yet realistic, presentation of each character in turn, the storyteller's concern is not so much in the historical aspect of his subject as it is in revealing human character and its effect on conduct. The characters of the saga have often great beauty and dignity. When his enemies burned Njal's house the women and children and house-carles were allowed, according to custom, to go out. But when it came the turn of Njal's wife, Bergthora, she replied "I was given away to Njal young, and I have promised him this, that we would both share the same fate." After that, Bergthora and Njal turned back into the burning house. Courage in the face of an adverse fate is the insistent, dominant note in the sagas. We find it again in the *Grettis Saga:*

> "We will meet our fate, whatever it may be," said Grettir. "And if our foes come against us, those shall not need to feel shame for the courage of thy sons . . . " Such was the death of Grettir, a man true to his word, and undaunted in spirit, and the strongest man that ever lived in Iceland.

It is inevitable that the heroic sagas of Iceland will have a strong interest for boys and girls. A child's mind is objective and grasps with ease the simple and positive code of an Icelander of the tenth century whose natural attitude toward life is that of pride and courage—pride in the man who does best the things with which all men are familiar, and courage above all. Yet while the sagas are, in their nature, of great interest to boys and girls, the very multiplicity of characters and incidents requires skilful adaptation in order to give the clearness and continuity necessary to hold the children's interest.

The Heroes of Iceland by Allen French is an adaptation of Dasent's translation of the saga of Burnt Njal and is actually an abridgment of Dasent, omitting all irrelevant episodes, minor incidents, and tedious genealogical information. In French's handling of the material the story retains its full force, its unity of conception, and its dramatic action. The real interest of boys and girls in this story of Gunnar and Njal is the adventurous lives they led. Here children find the material that feeds imagination, heroes that are genuine and significant, action of width and scope. The heroes themselves are of a kind that boys and girls appreciate to the full, men of great deeds and of undaunted courage in the face of insuperable odds. It is the kind of material which reaches beyond everyday life. To read it is to have a sense of heightened experience.

The unreluctant years

Allen French followed his adaptation of *Njal's Saga* with a retelling of William Morris' *Grettis Saga* which he called *The Story of Grettir the Strong*. This is not an abridgment but a retelling in his own words. Allen French understood the technique of the saga as it was developed in Iceland. He had studied the life, the beliefs, and the ideals of the Icelanders and he brings to his retelling the same spirit that informs the literature of the sagas. In his version, as in the original, events move forward in an inevitable sequence to a foreseen but inescapable tragic end.

The story of Grettir follows a single thread of biographical narrative: the life and adventures of a man outlawed through no fault of his own. Grettir—"the strongest man that ever lived in Iceland"—strides through the story like a giant among men, performing feats of superhuman strength and enduring great hardship and the loneliness of a man whom none dare befriend. Grettir's matter-of-fact heroism stands out against a mysterious background of fantasy in the account of the Hauntings at Thorhallstead, where he struggles with and overcomes the ghost of Glam. Allen French describes the conclusion of the struggle:

> There in the moonlight Grettir for the first time clearly saw Glam's face. So dreadful was the sight, with those huge eyes rolling horribly, that well-nigh Grettir's spirit fled, and he had no thought to save himself . . . But always after that Grettir saw strange shapes in the dark, and all sorts of horrors disturbed his sleep, and he could scarcely bear to be alone in the night.

This vividly told ghost story which explains Grettir's subsequent terror of the dark gives the *Grettis Saga* a romantic interest unlike other saga narratives, with the exception of the *Gisli Saga* which is also touched with fantasy. Grettir's later encounters with the troll-wife and the giant at the waterfall, and with the witch at Drangey, touch on the mystery of Grettir's life but do not obscure the tragic theme of the saga. Like Ulysses he was a man pursued by ill fortune, but unlike Ulysses, Grettir does not return triumphant:

> But in battle's crash,
> And mid the flash
> Of sword and spear
> —An outlaw's bier!

Allen French follows Grettir's last battle song with the simple statement "and therewith he died."

Although his version is based on William Morris' translation of the *Grettis Saga,* Allen French found Morris' poetic language and obscure archaisms unsuitable for his purpose. His retelling, while not distinguished in style, is nevertheless a clear, vivid, and spirited story that has integrity and a strong storytelling quality which makes it a natural introduction to the sagas for boys and girls.

The sagas of the Icelanders are drawn from the adventures of their local heroes. The *Saga of the Volsungs,* on the other hand, had its origin in Eddic heroic poetry although the saga form of the story was written down in Iceland in the thirteenth century by an unknown "saga man." William Morris translated the saga into English prose and then made a poetic paraphrase of the story in his famous narrative poem *The Story of Sigurd and The Fall of the Niblungs.*

Dorothy Hosford's retelling of the Volsung Saga for boys and girls, *The Sons of the Volsungs,* is based on the first two books of Morris' long poem, omitting the last two books which tell the Niblung story of betrayal and ultimate catastrophe. In the Hosford version the story ends with the great deeds of Sigurd's youth: the slaying of the dragon Fafnir on the glittering heath, and the awakening of Brynhild on fire-ringed Hindfell. There is a natural completeness to this ending, while the final sentence of the story is suggestive of further reading to the curious child:

> Such are the tales that are told of Volsung, and of Sigmund his son, and of Sigurd, who was mightiest of them all. More befell Sigurd in the days that were to come, both of grief and of joy, but these were the deeds of his youth.[1]

A retelling of the Volsung Saga presents all the problems inherent in any attempt to adapt the saga literature of Iceland for children. In addition to the usual problems, a prose retelling of a narrative poem such as *The Story of Sigurd* with its vehement beat, often obscure diction and archaic expressions, adds complexity to the other difficulties of a reteller. There is, for instance, the gradual working away from the verse form and the substitution of rhythmic prose for rhymed lines. There is, too, the stirring music of Morris' poetry that requires, in retelling, "the slow fine toil of getting all the lovely words just right" so that the heightened quality of Morris' heroic verse will not be lost in commonplace expression.

[1] Dorothy Hosford, *Sons of the Volsungs* (N.Y.: Holt, 1949), p.171. This and the quotations on pages 92 and 93 are used by permission.

The unreluctant years

William Morris put, perhaps, his finest poetry into the telling of *Sigurd the Volsung*. The story moves so that the balance is held between the action and its significance to the general theme. Volsung, Sigmund, and Sigurd are not supernatural beings although their deeds are shown against a background of mystical wonder. They are men whose characters stand out in clearness and strength as the story sweeps on. The poem has a spaciousness beyond the immediate scene, and a significance behind the stirring action which gives it epic quality.

Such a story may be retold in many ways. Dorothy Hosford, in *Sons of the Volsungs*, has caught and interpreted the epic quality that has made the story live through many centuries—that quality which makes it a good story in itself, but even greater in its significance. As she tells it, the tale never halts but moves forward in the irresistible way of all good storytelling; but at the same time there is, in the telling, an indefinable undertone which makes it more than a good story and which illuminates its action, characters, and meaning. When the daughter of Volsung—"Signy, the fairer than fair, Signy, the wiser than wise"— is given in marriage to the King of the Goths whose evil intent is known to her, she takes leave of her kindred with a burdened heart:

> The gangways were shipped, the last horn of farewell sounded as the wind filled the striped sails and the long-ship, carrying Signy, was borne out to sea. White and fair she stood among the glittering war shields, but her heart was closed on her grief, and not once did she look back to the land which little by little faded into the distance behind her.

It is only rarely that in a retelling a writer is able to give a sense of his own feeling for the wonders he is relating in a way that enhances rather than dims the heroic quality of the original. Charles Kingsley brought to the writing of *The Heroes* his knowledge of man's capacity for joy and sorrow, loyalty and betrayal, strength and weakness, cowardice and courage. Dorothy Hosford in her writing gives the reader the same sense of recognition and of understanding, in those faraway lives about which she tells.

The deeds of the heroes of *Sons of the Volsungs* are simple and stirring; but forthright and uncomplicated as they are, there is a sense of larger issues in the background—of ancient wisdom and the unknown ways of the future. Sigurd wins his horse and his sword, meets his foes and fights his battles, but what he is ultimately seeking is not glory but wisdom. "What then shall endure to tell the tale of the world?"

Sigurd asks Fafnir, the dreadful dragon whom he alone of all men has conquered. Sigurd moves through every enterprise and danger with steadfast courage and nobility of spirit, knowing that he fulfills a destiny shaped for him by universal forces far greater than himself. Sigurd is a great hero; but in his conception of himself as the instrument of forces beyond his control or understanding, or that of any man, he is also human. It is this that gives him character and a kind of reality that the reader is quick to recognize and respond to.

The poetic prose and rhythmical cadence of Dorothy Hosford's telling of the story heightens the exciting action and brings out the nobility of its conception. Brynhild's words to Sigurd on the mountain top before they turned "and went the roads that go green to the dwellings of men" round out this tale of the Volsungs to a memorable close:

> And she told of the hidden matters whereby the world is moved: she told of the framing of all things, the houses of the heaven, the star worlds' courses, and how the winds be driven. She told of the Norns and their names, and the fate that abideth the earth. She told of the ways of the king folk, of the love of women, of the fall of mighty houses, of the friend that falters and turns, and the grief that endureth for long.
>
> "Aye," she spake, "but man shall bear and forbear, and be master of all that is; man shall measure it all, the wrath, and the grief, and the bliss.
>
> ". . . Yet is each man wise to do bravely and well that thing that the Gods have given him to do."

Hero stories belong to that permanent kind of literature which represents the ideals and the way of thinking of the heroic age of the people with whom they originated. They reflect a temper of mind rather than a time; and this is the reason we put together in one company Odysseus and Grettir, Sigurd and Beowulf, Roland and King Arthur, Finn and Cuchulain. For although the deeds that are sung of one hero are different from those of another, their explanation is seen to be ultimately alike.

The strong appeal of these stories to boys and girls lies not alone in their adventure but also in their imaginative reality. They possess an inner core of truth—a meaning—which sets them apart from all other kinds of adventure stories; a significance to life not found in a story for children of invented characters and plot. No other kind of reading can give children an approximation to the imaginative experience and satisfaction that an adult reader gains from a great book such as, for instance, *War and Peace* or *King Lear*.

Fairy tales also have a kind of imaginative reality, and if a child has not known them in his earlier reading, he will be less ready to accept the conventions of the hero story. One difference between these two kinds of traditional literature is that in fairy tales the hero is sure to triumph in the end; but in hero stories boys and girls meet the good man who is faced by a hard choice, or who is pursued by ill fortune, or who makes one fatal mistake. The hero's triumph is not material: it is his courage that matters. He moves in a world of high ideals, but of everyday, though sometimes very grim, difficulties, mishaps, and human failings.

Children are aware, consciously or unconsciously, that in hero stories they find experience. Beyond their glamour and magic and romance there is something tough and real. In a story such as *Treasure Island* they meet a boy whose adventures they share with breathless excitement; but in *Grettir the Strong* they not only share his adventures, but his suffering and struggle win their sympathy and their respect. He becomes their friend, more real as a person to them than the hero of a fictional adventure story. When children have met and shared the life of a hero, life has more meaning to them than it could have had, had he never lived, or had his story never been told.

More and more of the literature of epic, saga, and romance is being made available for boys and girls in the form of retellings and adaptations. While all these require careful selection through comparison with the original source, it is not possible in so brief a survey to do more than indicate some basis of judgment in the case of a few of the stories, which can be applied toward the selection of the superior rather than the inferior versions of this kind of literature for children.

There is danger that because of the mass production of consciously designed "literature for children" today, and through general adult indifference or lack of knowledge, hero stories may not reach the children who can most enjoy them. Walter Pater has told us "to know when oneself is interested as a first condition of interesting other people." The interest in such material of those who have to do with children and their books will ensure that boys and girls do not miss this kind of reading which opens the mind and heart to new horizons and contributes to the resources of the spirit.

ASSOCIATIVE READING

DIXON, W. MACNEILE. English Epic and Heroic Poetry. Dutton, 1912. Dent, 1912.

Grettis Saga. The Saga of Grettir the Strong, tr. from the Icelandic by G. A. Hight. Dutton, 1913. Dent, 1913. (Everyman's Library)

HOMER. The Iliad of Homer, done into English Prose by Andrew Lang, Walter Leaf, and Ernest Myers. Macmillan, 1883.

——. The Odyssey of Homer, done into English Prose by S. H. Butcher and Andrew Lang. Macmillan, 1921.

——. The Odyssey of Homer, tr. by George Herbert Palmer. Houghton, Mifflin, 1929.

KER, W. P. English Literature: Mediaeval. 6th ed. Thornton Butterworth, 1932. (Home University Library)

——. Epic and Romance; Essays on Mediaeval Literature. Macmillan, 1926.

MORRIS, WILLIAM. The Story of Sigurd the Volsung and The Fall of the Niblungs. Longmans, Green, 1923.

Njals Saga. The Story of Burnt Njal, tr. from the Icelandic by George Webbe Dasent. Dent, 1911. (Everyman's Library)

The Poetic Edda, tr. from the Icelandic with an introd. and notes by Henry Adams Bellows. American Scandinavian Foundation, 1926.

WOOLF, VIRGINIA. On Not Knowing Greek (in *Second Common Reader*). Harcourt, Brace, 1932.

CHAPTER SEVEN

That is one of the pleasures of reading—you may make any picture out of the words you can and will; and a poem may have as many different meanings as there are different minds . . . I chose what I liked best—those that, when I read them, never failed to carry me away, as if on a Magic Carpet, or in Seven League Boots, into a region of their own. When the nightingale sings, other birds, it is said, will sit and listen to him: and I remember very well hearing a nightingale so singing on a spray in a dewy hedge, and there were many small birds perched mute and quiet near. The cock crows at midnight; and for miles around his kinsmen answer. The fowler whistles his decoy for the wild duck to come. So certain rhymes and poems affected my mind when I was young, and continue to do so now that I am old.

Walter de la Mare,
Come Hither

POETRY

Bright is the ring of words
   When the right man rings them,
Fair the fall of songs
   When the singer sings them.
Still they are carolled and said—
   On wings they are carried
After the singer is dead
   And the maker buried.

 It has been accepted by many unthinking people that poetry is purely imaginary "stuff" which has little to do with reality. But if the long poetic tradition, which has come down to us from the past, has a visible pattern, it is the pattern of life—the inner life of mind and heart, and the outer life of the world about us. It is the poet's intuition of the truth that lies at the heart of all life, and which through the medium of art he recreates in his imagination, that is the stuff of poetry.

Many people have tried to define poetry. Louis Untermeyer has quoted a number of these attempts in his anthology *Yesterday and Today,* yet it still eludes every effort to confine it, beyond argument, in a definition. Nor can we find a criterion which will prove for us that "this is poetry" or "this is not poetry." Although we cannot define poetry, we know that the word itself means making or creating; and the more creative energy there is found in a poem, the closer it approaches pure poetry, whether it be a single, sharp, clear, and moving image, as in Blake's "The Chimney-Sweeper," or the complex range of thought and feeling found in Keats' "Ode to a Nightingale."

The unreluctant years

The enjoyment of poetry, Robert Lynd tells us, is "not the possession of a select few but a part of the general human inheritance . . . we see the beginnings of it in the child's love of repetitions and rhythms . . ."[1] It seems only natural, then, that if we are eager to extend the children's spontaneous response to rhythm to the enjoyment of poetry itself, we will put into their hands the poetry which will give them the truest delight. Only in that way can we increase the number of children who turn to poetry with responsive minds and hearts.

What kind of poetry do children enjoy? In her introduction to *A Book of Famous Verse*, Agnes Repplier makes a few suggestions:

> The enjoyment which children receive from poetry is far-reaching and of many kinds. Martial strains which fire the blood, fairy music ringing in the ears, half-told tales which set the young heart dreaming, brave deeds, unhappy fates, sombre ballads, keen joyous lyrics, and small jeweled verses where every word shines like a polished gem,—all these good things the children know and love. It is useless to offer them mere rhymes and jingles; it is ungenerous to stint their young, vigorous imaginations with obvious prattle, fitted dexterously to their understandings. In the matter of poetry, a child's imagination outstrips his understanding; his emotions carry him far beyond the narrow reach of his intelligence. He has but one lesson to learn, —the lesson of enjoyment . . .

Through the beauty of some single poem read when they were children, many people must have heard for the first time the distant music of poetic beauty. It matters little what poem it was. It may have been the strange enchantment of "The Ancient Mariner" or the haunting refrain of "The Forsaken Merman" or the clear sharp image of

> Tiger, Tiger, burning bright
> In the forests of the night.

To such children it would seem that it only remained to give freedom to explore, and they would find their own way to the garden of the Hesperides.

Some children will always do their own exploring, intuitively following an inner compulsion toward all poetry. These are the children of acute and delicate perceptions who are able to give that intense attention which sheds a kind of incandescence on the poetry they read or hear. But although most children spontaneously respond

[1] Introduction to *An Anthology of Modern Verse*, ed. by A. Methuen (London: Methuen, 1921), p.xiii.

to verse from their first acquaintance with Mother Goose, many of them are early lured away. They may not be kept in touch with poetry, or it may be displaced by the more immediate appeal of "Little Red Riding Hood" and other stories told in the familiar speech of the prose narrative. What we do not always realize is that in almost all children the spontaneous response to poetry is not lost but rises eagerly to "the ring of words when the right man rings them."

Even writers of children's prose fiction have understood this as we see when we consider the occurrence of poetry in their stories. But although we know that a child's enjoyment of *Alice in Wonderland* is greater *with* the Mock Turtle's story than without it and that the *Wind in the Willows* would not be quite the same without the field mice's carol, this fugitive verse is secondary to the story that is told in these books. While it may quicken, it cannot sustain, a child's response to poetry. For reading poetry is not the same thing as reading a story. When we realize the difference and in what it lies, then we will begin to understand what poetry is and what it is not. We will come to understand, too, what children are looking for in the poem they read.

We have to remember that although poem and story are both made of words, the use made of them by poet and storyteller is different. A child who is familiar with the everyday words in common speech will readily follow "Cinderella" or "Puss in Boots" from "Once upon a time" to "they lived happily ever after." But when a child listens to poetry, he is becoming accustomed to words in an unfamiliar arrangement, or order; a use of words that gives him a different kind of pleasure from a story in prose; a pleasure that he finds in a poem like this:

> Oh, happy wind, how sweet
>   Thy life must be!
> The great proud fields of gold
>   Run after thee:
> And here are flowers, with heads
>   To nod and shake;
> And dreaming butterflies
>   To tease and wake,
> Oh, happy wind, I say,
> To be alive this day.[2]

or like this one, translated from the old English and called "The Swan":

[2] W. H. Davies, *Collected Poems* (London: Cape, 1928), p.89. Quoted by permission of Mrs. W. H. Davies and the publishers, Jonathan Cape ltd.

The unreluctant years

> My robe is noiseless while I tread the earth,
> Or tarry 'neath the banks, or stir the shallows;
> But when these shining wings, this depth of air,
> Bear me aloft above the bending shores
> Where men abide, and far the welkin's strength
> Over the multitude conveys me, then
> With rushing whir and clear melodious sound
> My raiment sings. And like a wandering spirit
> I float unweariedly o'er flood and field.[3]

With these cadences in his ears would any child be unresponsive to the rhythmic spell of poetic beauty? Yet this different use of words by the poet makes a different kind of demand upon the reader. It asks for a heightened attention perhaps similar to that he gives to music—a listening to the *sound* of words, the measured movement of their cadence—not because poetry is sound only but because the poet chooses and arranges words whose sound as well as whose meaning induces a mood sensitive and receptive to beauty—to music. A child is more easily persuaded to take pleasure in poetry through the tune of words, through his senses. It does not matter if the meaning is implicit in the sound. It is even more true of a child than of a grown-up that, as Coleridge says, "Poetry gives much pleasure when only generally, and not perfectly, understood."

Walter de la Mare has perceived that it is the incantation of verse which tempts the children to listen. In one of his anthologies of poetry for children he has something of his own to say about the poems they have just heard and draws them on, conversationally, to "fresh woods and pastures new." If we open *Tom Tiddler's Ground* we can listen as he talks to the children. He says this about Shelley's "The Question":

> The *sounds* of the words of poetry resemble the sounds of music. They are a pleasure and delight merely to listen to, as they rise and fall and flow and pause and echo—like the singing of birds at daybreak or a little before the fall of night when the daffodils "take the winds of March with beauty." It is a great pleasure also to *say* the words aloud—as well and clearly and carefully as one possibly can: "Green cowbind and the moonlight coloured may," or "flowers azure black and streaked with gold." Try it.

Listen as he tells them at the beginning of Wordsworth's "The Pet Lamb" that "this is only the beginning of a much longer poem, and a

[3]Walter de la Mare, *Tom Tiddler's Ground* (London: Collins, n.d.) by permission of Walter de la Mare.

very beautiful one too—with all the faint colours and the quiet of evening. But the rest can easily be found if you wish to read it." And this, at the end of Lewis Carroll's "Beautiful Soup": "This rhyme should be sung—with plenty of expression, especially on the beau-ootiful—to the tune of 'Star of the Evening.' It is one of the shorter rhymes out of *Alice in Wonderland,* and the next is a long one out of *Alice Through the Looking-Glass.* Both books were written by Lewis Carroll, and there are very few books I should be sorrier never to have read . . ."

Tom Tiddler's Ground "is only a little book" De la Mare tells us. "It gives only a glimpse of the great feast of English poetry. But that is much." How "much" it is must always depend on the choice that is given to children from the "great feast." Poetry, unlike other forms of literature, is common ground for both children and grown-ups. But since childhood is brief and since there is much poetry that waits on experience, it is, I think, generally conceded that anthologies for children offer the widest range for individual response. Let us therefore consider some of the qualities of the best anthologies.

Anyone who has read poetry to a receptive child and has seen the surprise of beauty dawn in young eyes knows how rewarding a labor of love the making of an anthology for children must be. Though a rewarding task, the making of an anthology is not an easy one. Not all anthologists can achieve it without repeating what others have done, or without condescension, or banality. Not everyone can gather the flowers of poesy with the sensitive feeling of an artist when he places in their right relation to color, form, and pattern, the flowers in a still life. Perhaps it takes a poet to work this miracle, just as it requires an artist to select the objects and then arrange them if a still life is to give pleasure to the eye. It has proved true, in any case, that the satisfaction we gain from an anthology is in proportion to the fusion in its making of the critical with the creative mind.

I suppose that anyone who sets out to make an anthology has some standard by which he tests the poems or verses before he is ready to include each one—some required degree of a quality or qualities which transcend everything else in the poem from his point of view as an anthologist. This point of view of the selector is what makes or mars his anthology and so should be understood before we can judge his success or failure in achieving his purpose. Let us consider from what viewpoint some children's anthologies have been selected.

The unreluctant years

Walter de la Mare tells us that in his anthologies he has gathered poetry that to his mind "wears well." I know of no criterion more demanding both of the poetry and the anthologist. The failure of too many collections of poetry for children lies in the lack of poems that wear well. To know whether a poem wears well one must have known it a long, long time. And to know whether it wears better than others so that it is chosen in preference to those others, assumes that the anthologist is a life-long reader of all poetry. There is implicit, too, that strong white light composite of imagination and memory turned full on the heart of childhood and its response to beauty. It is this *wearing* quality that heightens the delight that children find in the anthologies made by Walter de la Mare. In addition, his choice of poems reflects the imagination, the feeling for beauty and mystery, which are present in his own poetry.

One of the most winning aims an anthologist can have is stated by Kenneth Grahame in his preface to *The Cambridge Book of Poetry for Children.* He explains that his task is not to provide simple examples of the whole range of English poetry, "but to set up a wicket-gate giving attractive admission to that wide domain, with its woodland glades, its pasture and arable, its walled and scented gardens here and there, and so to its sunlit, and sometimes misty, mountain tops—all to be more fully explored later by those who are tempted on by the first glimpse."

Before Kenneth Grahame set up his "wicket-gate" so that children might enter and explore, he had refused admission to some kinds of poetry which do not belong, he thinks, in the children's "wide domain." The restrictions that he imposed on his choice of poetry for an anthology are both interesting and instructive to those who wish to know what he thought one should shun in choosing poems children will like.

Kenneth Grahame tells us that he avoided blank verse and the whole field of drama, though he gave admission to the fairy poetry and songs from Shakespeare's plays. Seventeenth and eighteenth century poetry, because of its classical form and classical allusions, he believed might well be left for riper years. Archaic language and dialect were barred, since Kenneth Grahame was reluctant to confuse a child's often painful acquirement of normal spelling. Certain subjects, such as death, he thought unsuitable for children's poetry, though he found that a surprising proportion of verse written for children was about "dead fathers and mothers, dead brothers and sisters, dead uncles and aunts, dead

102

puppies and kittens, dead birds, dead flowers, dead dolls."

Kenneth Grahame rejected all this obituary verse, preferring to give children poetry that sings of the joy of being alive. He rejected, too, verse which was merely verse, lacking any creative spark; and, finally, verse *about* children. The retrospective quality of the latter, he felt, was an adult interest, rather than one of childhood.

Having thus set down what he will not include, Kenneth Grahame surveys the final outcome: "All these restrictions have necessarily led to two results," he tells us. "First, that this collection is chiefly lyrical . . . The second result is that it is but a small sheaf that these gleanings amount to."[4]

An examination of other anthologies for children, those of Louis Untermeyer, for example, reveals that of the three great styles of poetry, the dramatic, the narrative, and the lyric, it is lyric poetry that forms by far the greater part of these collections. The reason, of course, is that dramatic and narrative poems, though they sometimes tell a story, are often of great length. Some of them, too, are concerned with philosophic, political, or historical ideas beyond the experience and knowledge of children. From one or other of these standpoints such poems as Milton's *Paradise Lost*, Byron's *Childe Harold,* or Hardy's *Dynasts* are obviously not wise choices, and can be left for a riper age.

While so much of the poetry included in anthologies for children is lyric, let us look first of all at another kind of poetry which anthologists seldom disregard—the ballads. "What is a ballad?" asks W. P. Ker, and continues: "A ballad is 'The Milldams of Binnorie' and 'Sir Patrick Spens' and 'The Douglas Tragedy' and 'Lord Randal' and 'Childe Maurice,' and things of that sort."[5] The ballads are hard to define or to place under any one of the three styles, the narrative, the dramatic, and the lyric since they combine some of the qualities of all three. Concerning their history we only know that they are almost the earliest poetry produced in England and Scotland and the Border, but who made them, and how, we can only surmise. Created as they were in the youth of the world, they appeal to "something young in the national mind." Ballads are, of course, historically interesting to students of English poetry. But to children it is the simplicity and effectiveness of the form of the ballad story that charms the ear and catches the

---

[4] Kenneth Grahame, ed., *The Cambridge Book of Poetry for Children* (N.Y.: Putnam, 1933), p.xiii-xiv.
[5] W. P. Ker, "On the History of the Ballads," *Proceedings of the British Academy,* Vol. IV.

imagination. They afford a natural avenue by which children can travel from stories in prose to stories in verse, and so into the whole literature of poetry.

Ballads resemble folk tales in the diversity of stories they tell—of the greenwood, of border raids and battles long ago, of love and death and sorcery. They are like folk tales, too, in the familiar characteristic of simple repetition that is common to both. The repetition often takes the form of a refrain as in "The Golden Vanity," in which the first and third lines develop the story as a kind of rhymed couplet, while the second and fourth lines form the refrain:

> There was a gallant ship, and a gallant ship was she,
>   Eck iddle du, and the Lowlands low;
> And she was called the Goulden Vanitie,
>   As she sailed to the Lowlands low.
>
> She had not sailed a league, a league but only three,
>   Eck iddle du, and the Lowlands low;
> When she came up with a French gallee
>   As she sailed to the Lowlands low.

Another form of repetition, called incremental, advances the story by having each stanza repeat the same situation but with a slight variation which carries the action further. "The Twa Sisters" is a characteristic example. Here are the last three stanzas:

> The first tune he did play and sing
> Was, "Farewell to my father the King."
>
> The nexten tune that he played syne,
> Was, "Farewell to my mother the Queen."
>
> The lasten tune that he played then,
> Was, "Wae to my sister, fair Ellen."

Not all ballads have a recurring chorus or refrain, or even the repetition of incident, characteristic of many of them; but like the folk tales they have come down to us in a recognizable and indestructible form of folk poetry, impossible to reproduce in the poetry of art. No one can write a modern folk tale; no one today can write a ballad that can be mistaken for the folk ballad; "folk" because they, both tale and ballad, were told and sung in a society where they were the common property of all, young and old, noble and peasant. There was no illiterate class since all were alike unlettered and the literature of the folk was equally accessible to all, and to all of similar interest. With the advance of civilization bringing knowledge of letters to a privileged class, the folk tales and ballads might have been forgotten had they not lived on in the hearts and minds—and tongues—of the simple, unlettered class who remained untouched by the developing intellectual life of the times.

While the folk tales are the antecedents of all prose narratives and while the ballads anticipated the development of the art of poetry, there is one great difference between them. The folk tales were *told*, while the ballads were *sung*, the tune weaving the spell of music into the words of the story in verse, stirring the emotions to deeper human feelings than are aroused by the narrative prose of the folk tale.

When we turn to lyric poetry, which forms so large a part of most anthologies for children, we turn but from the singing of a ballad to another kind of music, the tune of words. Even the meaning of the word lyric is derived from music, and any definition of it must fall back on the old canon that its structure is music and imagination.

Children respond to rhythm and sound from their earliest memories of chanting

> Hickory, dickory dock,
> The mouse ran up the clock
> The clock struck one,
> The mouse ran down,
> Hickory, dickory dock.

And it is to nursery rhymes such as this that Robert Lynd says, in his introduction to *An Anthology of Modern Verse,* many children owe "their first literary thrill." No one will deny that in addition to their inimitable cadence, or perhaps because of it, nursery rhymes have the quality of memorableness, an attribute that is a common factor in all forms of good literature.

A child's eager readiness for the tune of words in Mother Goose is continued in his playtime games as he becomes familiar with the counting-out rhymes and singing games which have become the inheritance of each successive generation of children. Considering the ease with which all this traditional verse becomes part and parcel of every child's literary luggage which he carries through life, we cannot but be aware of the simple fact that early influences, whatever they may be, have a permanence in relation to a child's impressionability. This permanence argues, surely, that the poetry by which his first

105

impressions are formed should be of a kind to "haunt the memories of later years with beauty."

Children respond eagerly to the tune of words in poetry itself, as well as in nursery rhymes and singing games. Lyric poetry, in essence, is music and imagination. It pictures the wonder and beauty of the natural world; the trees, flowers, birds, and animals, the sights, sounds, and scents, *freshly* as a child sees them. This ability to communicate the wonder that underlies the familiar, the beauty in the commonplace, is the lyric poet's magical gift. Most lyrics are concerned with a single experience in which, as in music, meaning and feeling are inseparable. When Thomas Hardy wrote "The Fallow Deer at the Lonely House" he caught a momentary experience of beauty and significance so that we feel it, too:

> One without looks in tonight
>   Through the curtain-chink
> From the sheet of glistening white;
> One without looks in tonight
>   As we sit and think
>   By the fender-brink.
>
> We do not discern those eyes
>   Watching in the snow;
> Lit by lamps of rosy dyes
> We do not discern those eyes
>   Wondering, aglow,
>   Fourfooted, tiptoe.[6]

Line by line, the poet builds up the picture of the solitary house with its human warmth and security, while outside the solitary deer stands in the unearthly radiance of the "sheet of glistening white," looking in. Into this quiet familiar room has come a sense of strangeness, an awareness of the winter woods, the cold, and the wild things whose home is there. There has come too a startled realization of the momentary intrusion of the strange and beautiful into the familiar and commonplace of life. Romance is blended with realism.

Lyric poetry, by directing sustained attention on a single happening, gives the sensitive reader an intense experience of life. When thought and feeling are joined with music—the music of rhythm and words— we are moved to an awareness of what the poet is trying to express. It may be an intensely remembered event of the past, or perhaps an

[6] Thomas Hardy, *Collected Poems* (N.Y.: Macmillan, 1898), p.566.

immediate experience of the beauty and mystery of the world about us. Whatever it is, the degree of awareness that the poem requires of the reader is a measure of its lyric quality.

There are no rules that we can apply to a lyric poem, which, if it conforms, will prove it to be truly lyrical. Our sensitive response will tell us the degree of our liking for any poem; but before we can trust our intuitions should we not test our spontaneous susceptibility to poetry that is acknowledged to be the finest in the whole literature of poetry? In judging any poem we have no way of knowing what our standard of judgment is unless we refer it to what is generally accepted as great poetry. In the last lecture that Kenneth Grahame gave he said that "after all, the things that really matter are quite definite. Sheer absolute merit, sheer quality is definite. When we open a certain book at random, and come upon such a passage as:

> Night's candles are burnt out, and jocund day
> Stands tiptoe on the misty mountain tops . . .

we don't argue, we *know*. We just say to ourselves, 'well, there you are! That's *it!*' "[7]

This recognition whereby our intuition tells us that "this is poetry" or "this is not," is measured, not only by the poem we read, but by the range of sympathy, the delicacy of perception we bring to our reading. We discover for ourselves what degree of awareness, of attention, the poem demands. The more heightened the demand on all our senses, the more we are moved. Better than anyone else, I think, Emily Dickinson has put into words the strange power of poetry to move us by the poet's use of words in a certain order, by musical rhythm, and by imagery, rich with suggestion, to a more intense experience than we have ever known. Emily Dickinson says:

> If I read a book and it makes my whole body so cold no fire can ever warm me, I know that is poetry. If I feel physically as if the top of my head were taken off, I know that is poetry. These are the only ways I know it. Is there any other way?

Every lyric poet has his own kind of music and his own intuitions of beauty and truth and his own way of communicating them. He may, as Coleridge says, "by a single word, perhaps, . . . instil that energy into the mind which compels the imagination to produce the picture . . ."

[7] Kenneth Grahame, "A Dark Star," in Patrick R. Chalmers, *Kenneth Grahame* (London: Methuen, 1923).

The unreluctant years

When Blake writes of a lost emmet

> Troubled, 'wildered and forlorn
> Dark, benighted, travel-worn

or of night

> The moon, like a flower
> In Heaven's high bower,
> With silent delight
> Sits and smiles on the night.

or of a bird

> Yonder stands a lonely tree
> There I live and mourn for thee
> Morning drinks my silent tear
> And evening winds my sorrow bear.

or of joy in nature

> When the green woods laugh with the voice of joy,
> And the dimpling stream runs laughing by;

the music and meaning of the lines are so blended that we are carried imaginatively into the experience the poet is trying to picture.

On the other hand we are not apt to be moved by lines that merely put in rhyme the commonplaces, untouched by beauty, that could have been said as well in prose, for, as George Macdonald asks

> How shall he sing who hath no song?
> He laugh who hath no mirth? . . .

Yet because of popular misunderstanding of a child's capacity for wonder and delight, how often he is offered the matter-of-fact rhymes of songless writers of "children's verse" instead of the music and imagination of the true lyric poetry to which his spirit is attuned!

What kind of poetry do children like? Forrest Reid believes that since children are individuals, as their elders are individuals, with varying minds and temperaments, "nobody can possibly tell what will sing its way into a child's spirit, set alight some flame of his imagination."[8]

In a round childish hand on the title page of a library copy of *Come Hither* were written the words "a good book, believe me." In the same hand were found comments on individual poems which had "set alight some flame of his imagination." The comments, and the poems to which they were joined were these:

[8] Forrest Reid, *Walter de la Mare, a Critical Study* (London: Faber, 1929), p.27.

108

Song on May Morning "beautiful"
Tell Me Where Is Fancie Bred "good"
When That I Was and a Little Tinie Boy "great"
When Isicles Hang by the Wall "funny"
Lucifer in Starlight "he is smart" "good"
The Twa Sisters "nice"
A Verse Found in Sir Walter Raleigh's Bible "wonderful"
Hush-a-ba, Birdie, Croon, Croon "beautiful verses"

Here is a child with a wide range of poetry set before him and he chooses an old ballad and an old rhyme, three of Shakespeare's songs, and poems by Sir Walter Raleigh, John Fletcher, John Milton, and George Meredith. Might this not suggest that it is well not to underestimate a child's spontaneous response to poetry, even though inarticulate in his comments, at an "age when the love of poetry may be born and strengthened"?

When it comes to this strengthening and developing of the appreciation of poetry, the value of poetry written *for* children has often been a matter of debate. There is the almost universal popularity of A. A. Milne's verses, *When We Were Very Young*, for instance. We find in them none of the vapid jog-trot, tedious and poverty stricken in imagination, which has brought much so-called poetry for children into disrepute. Instead, A. A. Milne "tells little stories in metre; and the dainty metres are handled with such ease that the child does not know that what he is hearing is 'poetry' at all—as of course it is not. He thinks he is hearing—as indeed he is—an amusing story told in sentences that are strangely dancing."[9] We have only to think of

> The King asked
> The Queen, and
> The Queen asked
> The Dairymaid:
> "Could we have some butter for
> The Royal slice of bread?"[10]

to find the gaiety and unexpectedness of the metre carrying us easily and gracefully to the end of the story. No one will deny its charm and originality, but will anyone maintain that it is poetry?

In order to understand what the verses of *When We Were Very*

[9] Henry Charles Duffin, *Walter de la Mare, a Study of His Poetry* (London: Sidgwick, 1944), p.132.
[10] "The King's Breakfast," from *When We Were Very Young*, Copyright, 1924, E. P. Dutton & Co., Inc. Renewed, 1952, A. A. Milne.

Young are, as well as what they are not, it is instructive to ask oneself
where may be found their counterpart in adult reading: when perhaps
the Gilbertian verses of *The Bab Ballads* will come to mind, or similar
lighthearted extravaganza in which we are at home in a world of
delicious fooling. Let us by all means give the children A. A. Milne
and Edward Lear and Hilaire Belloc "for fun" as these authors intended. But let us not make the mistake of thinking we are thereby
putting them under the influence of poetry.

There are many ways of writing in verse for children but, for the
purpose of this inquiry, the only way that is relevant is the way of
poetry. That thought immediately brings to our minds Walter de la
Mare's *Songs of Childhood,* and his other books for children to which
he has given such enticing titles: *Peacock Pie, Down-adown-derry,
Bells and Grass.*

It is possible to ask, though it may prove difficult to answer,
what is the content of a poet's mind, what the quality of "the shaping
spirit of imagination" which colors and directs all that he expresses
in poetry? The answer, of course, is best found in a study of his
writing and in the effect it produces on us. Let us look at one of
De la Mare's poems which he calls "Shadows." We realize as we read
that it has two intentions: first to evoke a picture; and second, to
express the range of the poet's thoughts in contemplating the scene.

The poem begins drowsily. We feel the hot noon sun beating down
on field and meadow. We hear the monotonous sounds of browsing
horses and the swishing of the cow's tail "plumb over its shadow . . ."
In the second verse, the point of observation shifts to "the old thorn
on the steep" where in its welcome shade a shepherd and sheep dog
sit watching their sheep. Then comes a vivid picture of beauty:

> It is cool by the hedgerow,
> A thorn for a tent,
> Her flowers a snowdrift,
> The air sweet with scent.

While our senses are lost in contemplation of fragrant loveliness,
the shadows slowly move. We are sharply recalled by the fourth
stanza:

> But oh, see already
> The shade has begun
> To incline to'rds the East,
> As the earth and the sun

> Change places, like dancers
> In dance: . . . [11]

Suddenly the poem takes on overtones of meaning that reach beyond the meadow to the wonder of the recurring rhythm of the universe —the music and mystery of the spheres.

It is this capacity to see "the rarest charm of familiarity in strangeness," the beauty of this earth in its relation to spiritual beauty, separated one from the other only by a veil of gossamer thinness, that is, I think, Walter de la Mare's quality. His poetry is compounded of imagination, vision, and dream, into which beauty breaks through when we least expect it. His mastery of flexible and subtle rhythms is so deft that it is, perhaps, hardly realized. Yet it sweeps us into the mood of the poem almost unaware. No one can read

> Ann, Ann!
> Come! quick as you can!

without feeling the urgency and excitement of the revelation about to be made. Nor can one miss the listening expectancy of

> Someone is always sitting there
> In the little green orchard;

and the clop, clop, rhythm of an old donkey's hoofs can be heard in

> Nicholas Nye was lean and grey
> Lame of leg and old.[12]

Perhaps the most subtle of all De la Mare's rhythms is found in "The Listeners"; a rhythm which Forrest Reid calls "syncopated":

> Is there anybody there? said the Traveller,
> Knocking on the moonlit door.[13]

and we stand, hesitating, in the moonlight, at one with the strange eerie mood the poem has evoked in the first line.

There has been discovered no process of analysis by which a poem can be taken apart to show why it is poetry or why it is not. It is something intensely felt or it is nothing. But it is possible to study

[11] *Bells and Grass* (N.Y.: Viking, 1942). This and the quotation from "Two Deep Clear Eyes" on p.112 are used by permission.

[12] The three preceding quotations and the one following from "The Song of the Secret" are from *Peacock Pie* (N.Y.: Holt, 1913).

[13] Walter de la Mare, from "The Listeners" in his *Collected Poems* (N.Y.: Copyright, 1920 by Henry Holt and Company, Inc. Copyright, 1948 by Walter de la Mare. Used by permission of the publishers.).

the devices a poet uses to obtain the effect he achieves even though
the devices are inherent in his poetic gift. Walter de la Mare says
that it is "one of every poet's loveliest devices with words—to let
the music of his verse accord with its meaning"; and that "loveliest
device" is his in greatest measure. It sounds in our ears like a tolling
bell in "The Song of the Secret":

> Where is beauty?
> Gone, gone:
> The cold winds have taken it
> With their faint moan;
> The white stars have shaken it,
> Trembling down,
> Into the pathless deep of the sea;
> Gone, gone
> Is beauty from me.

Reading his poems for children we find ourselves asking how it is
possible to reach to the other side of dream, and name the magical
spell that is De la Mare's own. We are at a loss for the identifying
word, but we are conscious of having discovered a touchstone by
which we can estimate how closely verses written for children
approach poetry. The influence of De la Mare's poetry on children
themselves is that of an awakening of minds, hearts, and imaginations to wonder, to a sense of beauty unseen, but waiting only on
the awareness of all the senses to reveal itself. And it is Walter de la
Mare who says to the children in his own words:

> Eyes bid ears
> Hark:
> Ears bid eyes
> Mark:
> Mouth bids nose
> Smell:
> Nose says to mouth
> I will:
> Heart bids mind
> Wonder:
> Mind bids heart
> Ponder.

Walter de la Mare makes no concessions to the popular idea that
poetry for children should be simplified or watered down. He

imposes no age levels. Instead, he trusts wholly to their intuitive response to wonder and beauty.

In giving poetry to children it is well to remember that they understand far more than they can express. Children apprehend by intuition and imagination that which is far beyond their limited experience. In their reading of true poetry, they are not only laying up a store of purest English, they are also finding an expresssion for thoughts and feelings of which they are but dimly aware. If our aim is to extend the number of children who turn to poetry expecting delight, it seems only natural that we must put within their reach the poetry whose power to delight is most present and most memorable.

The subject matter of poetry is both vast and elusive; its influence is incalculable. In so brief an inquiry into *what poetry for children,* only a few suggestions can be given. It is well to remember that there is no dividing line between poetry children like and poetry liked by adults, except that the very freshness and eagerness of their approach gives children the advantage. Children respond to the best and deserve the best, but we can only be sure that they receive it if we test what we offer them by reference to great poetry—or abide by the choice of those who are themselves poets.

ASSOCIATIVE READING

AUSLANDER, JOSEPH, and HILL, F. E. The Winged Horse. Doubleday, Doran, 1927.

CHILD, FRANCIS JAMES. English and Scottish Popular Ballads. Student's Cambridge ed. Houghton, Mifflin, 1904.

ECKENSTEIN, LINA. Comparative Studies in Nursery Rhymes. Duckworth, 1906.

HARTOG, Sir PHILIP JOSEPH. On the Relation of Poetry to Verse. Oxford Univ. Pr., 1926. (English Association Pamphlet no. 64)

HAZLITT, WILLIAM. On Poetry in General (in *Lectures on the English Poets*). Oxford Univ. Pr. (World's Classics)

HOUSMAN, ALFRED EDWARD. The Name and Nature of Poetry. Cambridge Univ. Pr., 1935.

OPIE, IONA, and OPIE, PETER, eds. The Oxford Dictionary of Nursery Rhymes. Clarendon Pr., 1951.

REID, FORREST. Walter de la Mare, a Critical Study. Holt, 1929.

SACKVILLE-WEST, V. Nursery Rhymes. Michael Joseph, 1950.

UNTERMEYER, LOUIS, and DAVIDSON, H. CARTER. Poetry, Its Appreciation and Enjoyment. Harcourt, Brace, 1934.

CHAPTER EIGHT

First impressions of pictures, rhymes and stories are both enduring and elusive . . . Here, to my mind, is the normal beginning of any true appreciation of art and of that folk feeling for other countries which fires the imagination. No country will ever seem entirely strange whose picture books have been familiar to us from childhood. Caldecott, Greenaway, Leslie Brooke, Boutet de Monvel, Walter Crane—best possible fortification against the vulgarity, the materialistic conceptions and cheap fancy which characterize many of the popular books for little children.

Fine picture books exert a far more subtle influence in the formation of reading tastes and habits than it is possible to estimate, for their integrity is unshakeable.

Anne Carroll Moore,
The Three Owls

PICTURE BOOKS

Little children live in the most private of all worlds. What wonderings and astonishments of delight and sorrow fill their thoughts and imaginations we cannot know and they have no words to tell. They learn to use words quickly or slowly, but the power to communicate their crowding impressions and the thoughts these evoke waits on understanding.

Our own intimations of a little child's mind and heart rise, it seems to me, from memory, imagination, and observation. Since each child is an individual, our aim in first introducing him to books must be to find some means of communication that is universal and continuous, that will meet a child's needs in his instinct toward growth.

A little child will express his pleasure in the rhythm of sound by beating time to the jingle of nursery rhymes and songs. This is his first realization of a rhythm and beat in language, and if kept alive is the beginning of a liking for poetry and music. The rhythmic movement of "Bye Baby Bunting" or "Hey Diddle Diddle" gives little children a physical sensation of pleasure even before they associate pleasure with the words of the rhyme or the tune of the song.

As it is with nursery rhymes—the substance of many picture books— so it is with picture books of all kinds. The most important approach is through the senses. Little children cannot read, and so their pleasure comes through their ears, through the rhythmic beat of language, through rhyme by means of sound, though not necessarily by the sense if we remember the charm of Johnny Crow:

> Till the Hippopotami
> Said: "Ask no further 'What am I?' "

Even if in prose, the sound of the sentences has much to do with a little child's pleasure in listening to a story. The more spaciousness and

115

shape given to the sentences the greater ease and balance there is to please the listening ear when they are read aloud.

Picture books also appeal to little children through the eye. But it is not, as with an adult, the appeal of aesthetic pleasure in the artist's line, color harmony, composition and style. A little child's approach to pictures is first of all a literary one. He expects them to tell him the story he cannot read for himself. Pictures are his first introduction to books and through them his interest is caught. If the story is there, his eyes will find it. Not long ago a boy sat down with his little brother and opened the pages of William Nicholson's *Clever Bill.* "You see, Tommy," he said, "you don't have to know how to read. Just turn the pages and the pictures will tell you the story."

What kind of picture books do little children like, and how are we to recognize, in this day of mass production, the picture book that is exceptional, distinctive, and pleasure-giving in the greatest degree? While picture books appeal primarily to the senses of little children, they appeal also to mind and emotion. But to interest a child the ideas and feelings they contain must be those of childhood and not merely simplified adult ideas and emotions. The picture book is a book in two media—words and paint, or whatever medium the artist uses. The text and pictures are of equal importance in considering a picture book as a whole, since it is the fusion of the two which gives the book its unity and character.

We are apt to generalize about little children's preferences and prejudices. We say they do not like black and white drawings, or that they like strong primary colors, or that they are "put off" by design. This seems a mistaken approach when we consider the fresh and eager expectation with which little children turn to their books. The truth is that they like the picture if it tells a story, whether it is drawn in black and white as in Wanda Gag's *Millions of Cats,* or in flat colors as in Marjorie Flack's *Angus and the Ducks,* or in the delicate water colors of *Peter Rabbit* or in the studied design of Walter Crane's *Bluebeard.*

What little children are looking for in a picture book is adventure; a story with the sort of pictures into which they can enter and take part in what happens to the hero, whether he is a puppy, a rabbit, a toy, a locomotive, or just a small boy like Little Jack Horner. The experience of life with which the story is concerned should be simple and un-complicated to keep within the range of a little child's understanding and imagination, though we must remember that these are constantly expanding and developing. If we are to learn how to judge the pictures of a picture book, it is essential to learn to see—to see with the eyes of a child the story the picture tells, and also to experience with the eyes of an adult the aesthetic pleasure of the illustrator's art.

The story in the picture is active in the degree that the artist's imagination is creative. In good picture books it is this ability to picture what is happening that gives the story greater vividness than it could have without the pictures. When a child's imagination is caught by what the picture tells him, he assimilates, as well, the whole picture. If it is a good picture, he has unconsciously absorbed an aesthetic experience which, if often repeated, will develop in him a standard of taste—a protection from the merely inferior, the shoddy and the mediocre.

The difference between a good picture and a bad one is, like beauty, in the eye of the beholder. The trained eye is the one that has learned to see pictures through looking at many that are known to be great art, through comparing them with other pictures. In this way it becomes possible to see into the mind of the artist and to read what he is saying through the strokes of his brush or pencil. The way he says it is his style, the personal expression of his temperament and idea. His success, in the case of the picture-book artist, rests primarily in integrating the pictures with the action of the story so that a life-giving and memorable unity is achieved.

Art is not simple, and the most seemingly artless picture book may have years of study behind the form in which we see it. But the recognition of its art demands, of those who would learn to know good pictures from poor ones, familiarity with and feeling for the work of artists of many kinds from the classical to the experimental. Do not the colored drawings of Paris in Bemelmans' *Madeline* evoke the suggestion of more than one serious influence, Vlaminck for instance, lighthearted though they are and not serious in themselves?

Simply to open one of the beautiful picture books of today is for most adults an experience of aesthetic pleasure. The artist's craftsmanship excites our enthusiasm and admiration. But little children have a different criterion. There are picture books published each year which beguile an adult with their color, design and form. Their excitement or wit or fancy make us exclaim and smile and wonder. Yet the little children for whom they are designed may look at them with inattention and indifference, even if at first their natural eager expectation of delight carries them through the book—once. When they do not find what they are looking for, they turn aside to tried favorites with the certainty of remembered joy and laughter. Perhaps a study of the picture books to which little children return again and again will give us the clue we need to recognize what it is in the pictures which satisfies the demands of little children.

We take for granted, today, the beautiful picture books that come from the press in such bountiful supply. But their tradition is a short one in comparative terms. The first modern picture books, as we know them, appeared in the last quarter of the last century. With them are indissolubly associated the names of Walter Crane, Kate Greenaway and Randolph Caldecott.

These three, working in quite different styles though contemporaries, produced the first picture books of the modern kind. They were the most beautiful that had ever been seen, and to some "connoisseurs of pleasure" they still are. Of the three, Walter Crane was the most serious in artistic intention. In *An Artist's Reminiscences* he tells us that while his picture books did not bring him much money, being sold outright to the publishers for a modest sum, nevertheless "I had my fun out of them, as in designing I was in the habit of putting in all sorts of subsidiary detail that interested me, and often made them the vehicle for my ideas in furniture and decoration."

Walter Crane explains in his own words his choice of picture books as a vehicle for his interest in design: "In a sober and matter of fact age they afford the only outlet for unrestricted flights of fancy to the modern illustrator who likes to revolt against the despotism of facts." His preoccupation with decoration is more marked in some of his picture books than in others. When his "flights of fancy" have caught the dramatic situations of the story he is most successful. His knack of telling a story in pictures captivates children and he creates a convincing fairyland of splendor and enchantment which overcomes a child's instinctive aversion to formalized design.

The detail in any one of Walter Crane's pictures seems inexhaustible and is a rewarding study in unity for any adult. In his *Bluebeard* picture book we see a furtive wife, fatal key in hand, gliding down a golden staircase. She is pictured in a flowing pre-Raphaelite gown stealing away from her guests who are examining gilded chests, Grecian pottery, and an ornate dressing table. Behind the figure of the wife is pictured the suggestive allegory of Eve with an arm outstretched to the apple on a formalized tree. The open doorways that recede further and further into the picture are typical of Walter Crane's faculty of appealing to the imagination in their suggestion of unseen but inexhaustible treasure beyond the immediate picture. More than others, his pictures seem to say to a child, "Once upon a time, in a far country . . ."

Walter Crane's picture books are an education in line, color, and design. His colors are warm and jewel-like, the orange making a glowing contrast against the subdued blue. He composes his pictures so that the lines of the garments and the direction of the figure's glance lead the eye to the action that is taking place in the picture. His composition is interesting, too, in its use of pillars and archways to frame important characters in the story, making them stand out against the wealth of detail and the rich background.

Some of Walter Crane's most serious work is found in the black and white drawings he made for Grimm's *Household Tales* for which his sister, Lucy Crane, translated the stories. The permanent and undisputed place of this collaboration in children's literature suggests that Walter Crane's fairy-tale picture books might also have survived to the present day if the text of the stories, instead of the versions he chose, had been equal in strength to his illustrations. The fact that his *Baby's Opera* and *Baby's Bouquet,* with their traditional songs set to simple traditional tunes by Lucy Crane, are as indispensable today as when they were published lends point to the need for strength equally in pictures and text if a picture book is to give lasting pleasure.

The art of Kate Greenaway's picture books, her critics say, is not to be analyzed, but enjoyed. In one of his lectures John Ruskin said:

> Observe that what this impressionable person *does* draw she draws as like as she can. It is true that the combination or composition of things is not what you see every day. You can't every day, for instance, see a baby thrown into a basket of roses; but when she has once pleasantly invented that arrangement for you, baby is as like baby and rose as like rose as she can possibly draw them. And the beauty of them is in being like, they are blissful just in the degree that they are natural; the fairy-land that she creates for you is not beyond the sky nor beneath the sea, but near you, even at your doors. She does but show you how to see it, and how to cherish.

119

The unreluctant years

Kate Greenaway's pictures for *Under the Window, Marigold Garden, A Child's Day* and all her other picture books are filled with natural, happy children dressed in quaint high-waisted square-necked frocks, muslin caps, wide bonnets, little aprons and breeches—playing games, dancing, walking or merely dreaming in childish revery. Her picture children are shown against delicate spring-like landscapes of old cottages with formal gardens or farmhouses set in fields of bloom. Part of the charm of her pictures is their effortless, unstudied look as well as the gay yet delicate color. The verses which accompany the pictures are her own, and without pictures would have little to commend them to succeeding generations. Without the inversions they would be little more than a running comment in prose, and in their verse form they often lack both rhythm and good rhyme. Although her pictures have little forceful activity, sensitive children are drawn to Kate Greenaway's books by the strength of her affectionate and understanding portrayal of what Austin Dobson called "the coy reticences, the simplicities and the small solemnities of little people" and by the fresh beauty of her flowers and gardens.

To look at Randolph Caldecott's picture books is to find oneself in gay and lively company. His unfailing humor, his affectionate, observant interest in animals and his robust lighthearted enjoyment of the out-of-doors are found in all of his sixteen picture books for children. Kate Greenaway was fascinated on seeing some of his sketches for nursery rhymes. "They are uncommonly clever," she wrote. "The dish running away with the spoon—you can't think how much he made of it." Caldecott's apparently inexhaustible fancy playing with the concluding light words of the rhyme pictures the dish as a dashing beau running off with a coy feminine spoon, while through the open door the cat is seen fiddling to the dancing of the china dishes. Even the plates standing on the plate rail jig merrily to the music. When we turn the page, the dish and the spoon, looking very pleased with themselves, are resting on a bench before resuming their flight. But in the next picture the gallant plate has come to grief and lies shattered on the floor, while an unrelenting father knife and a haughty mother fork march away between them a crestfallen daughter spoon.

A few words will supply Caldecott with ideas for many pictures. His pictured comments are not only on the bare text. His imagination seizes on all the successive steps, both before and after any situation, and on the byplay of minor as well as major characters who may or may not be mentioned in the text. It is as if he is saying to the children, "Look, this is how it all happened."

Caldecott's strength, which is the weakness of both Walter Crane and Kate Greenaway, is his power to give personality to both human and animal characters. His pen and ink sketches, often overlaid with bright but not gaudy color, are a study in expression with a minimum of line. Whether it is amusement, dejection, deference, disapproval, expansiveness or recoil, his drawing makes every emotion unmistakable and graphic. His nursery-rhyme picture books are full of action, humor and fancy and show to a high degree that essential quality of storytelling.

The diversity of style and subject among these three innovators of the fine picture book has continued in the whole tradition of picture books to the present day. The subject matter of picture books varies from the serious to the hilarious and from the factual to the completely fantastic. The styles of the creative illustrators are their own and their differences are wide. The picture books of Leslie Brooke are of special note. The tradition begun with Randolph Caldecott has been carried a step further in *Ring o' Roses, Johnny Crow's Garden* and *The Golden Goose Book.* Leslie Brooke has the same capacity as Caldecott for seeing with the eyes of a child. He has a similar gift of unfailing fancy and lively humor. And, like Caldecott, his pictures are full of activity in dramatic happenings.

What could be more expressive than his pictures for "The Three Little Pigs"? On the first page we see them leaving home to seek their fortunes, airy, self-confident and eager to appear worldly-wise. On the final page we find the single survivor, grown to be a cautious and wise little pig, as he sits snug and complacent in the little house made of bricks. Family portraits adorn the walls, and before the hearth is spread a rug made from the skin of the wicked wolf. Leslie Brooke's memorable pictures make us laugh as we see, for instance, the look of gratified pride with which Mother and Father Bear watch the small bear turning somersaults in the garden, or the expectant expression of the pig in "This little pig had roast beef," or the jauntiness, touched with apprehension, due perhaps to the feather, in "the Rat who wore a Feather in his Hat" in "Johnny Crow's Garden."

Leslie Brooke draws creatures familiar to children and shows them in such unexpected circumstances, drawn with such particularity of

121

detail, that they acquire an exciting freshness and romance to children. He never forgets children's affection for animals, and his appreciation of their comic traits is always warm and friendly. Leslie Brooke's, perhaps more than most picture books, belong to all childhood, not just to one generation alone. Like the nursery rhymes and fairy tales he illustrates, his picture books are ageless and timeless.

If Leslie Brooke is to us, in some aspects, a reincarnation of Caldecott, Beatrix Potter reminds us of Kate Greenaway in her delicate water colors of the English countryside, its pastures, its lanes and hedgerows full of flowers and birds. But there the resemblance ceases. The characters on the pages of Beatrix Potter's miniature volumes are not children in old-world costume but rabbits and ducks, squirrels, mice and other small animals of the fields and woods. She dresses them smartly in red hoods and blue jackets and tells their story in pictures and in a simple direct text that is clear and vigorous. Her words are chosen for their fitness to express the story as concisely as possible and the pictures they suggest.

Simply as the stories are told, they are not oversimplified, nor are they without subtlety. They are within the limits of a little child's world, yet provide plenty of scope for his imagination. While the adventures Beatrix Potter relates are woven of her original fancy, they remain plausible because they are based on the native characteristics of the animal of whom she writes. In *Jemima Puddleduck,* for example, the plot centers around the natural instinct of ducks to hide their nests. Foxes are known to eat ducks, dogs will hunt foxes. There we have the complete basis for the plot of the story.

The conversation allowed to the animal characters is sparing and is in every case characteristic of the particular animal's temperament. Addlepated Jemima Puddleduck flutters and mumbles her words and her conversation is of the vague kind that indicates her flighty and confused mind. On the other hand, Mr. Fox's speech is inclined to grandiloquence; the suave eloquence of his words is in keeping with his devious nature. Not only do the animals talk in character, they also act in the same way.

It is in those places where the behavior of the characters varies from the usual that we discover the humorous touches in Beatrix Potter's picture books. Her humor, never hilarious, is quiet and insinuating. Jemima is devoid of humor in herself but looks ridiculous flying through the air in full regalia. Mr. Fox puts his tail in his pocket so that Jemima will not be needlessly alarmed, and he winks at the child, to let him in on the secret plan, as he closes the door of his summer residence.

Beatrix Potter's illustrations are inseparable from her stories. They are integrated to give a single and memorable experience. The pictures are composed not only with a sense of story detail but with a background which gives aesthetic pleasure. When Jemima sets out "along the cart road that leads over the hill" Beatrix Potter shows us the low hills, the rambling stone fence, and in the distance the woods coming into leaf; the whole suffused with the faint, pink haze of an English spring. All her pictures make a profound, if unconscious, impression on a child's taste and influence his development.

The text of Beatrix Potter's books has a background of natural history which is within a little child's comprehension or intuitive appreciation, though not necessarily within his limited experience. For instance, Jeremy Fisher's home life is different from, but analogous to, that of any child. The difference gives it allure and interest while the similarity relates it to experience. The characteristics of these small animals are transposed into human terms, but the natural enmities between animals remain. Although these are kept a minor part of the story, they illustrate the author's intimate knowledge of the small animals of which she writes, and her integrity in the use of that knowledge.

Beatrix Potter creates a world in miniature in her little picture books. It is a world scaled to the comprehension of a little child's mind and imagination, which yet possesses fundamental truth. With their neat economy of phrase the stories are a joy to read aloud; and the accompanying pictures with their expressive characterization of small animals and their background of the English lake district pictured in affectionate detail, perfectly interpret the stories. Beatrix Potter's stories and pictures of small animals have been imitated, but never have they been surpassed.

As we look back on the work of these illustrators of the late nineteenth and early twentieth centuries, and as we examine the illustrations of their contemporaries in England, in Europe, and in America, we are more than ever aware of the altered aspect of picture books today. The change became marked in the period between the two world wars. Many artists from Western Europe were drawn to American shores in order to escape from the unrest of their homelands, torn with economic and political strife. As a result of this migration, the picture book in America became enriched by the fusion of many traditions of art with those of American-born artists who in turn had their own traditions. This commingling of cultures, further enriched by the importation of picture books from abroad, has resulted in a diversity and an abundance of picture books never achieved before, nor elsewhere.

The variety we find in contemporary picture books is not only in subject, but in expression. Picture books reflect to some extent the artistic ideas and styles of their time. What could be more natural than that the self-expressionism of the artists of today is found in the illustrations of our modern picture books? Each illustrator has his individual way of drawing the picture as he sees it in his mind. He is original to the degree in which he sees it freshly, in a new way that kindles imagination.

The modern picture book has often a Continental sophistication and sense of design that give it style as well as originality. Different in their exciting variety as one picture book is from another, their power to charm the heart of childhood is not in their diversity. Neither are children aware that many traditions of Continental and American art have influenced the picture books they enjoy today. It is undeniable that the art of the illustrator can give a child an experience of aesthetic pleasure, but only, I think, when a child absorbs a picture in its entirety because the story and the picture taken together are a single, vital experience into which he can easily enter.

If we read and look at a few of these twentieth-century picture books that little children have taken to their hearts—which they (or their parents to them) read and re-read again and again, finding in them endless delight and satisfaction, we shall discover why some picture books have this timeless quality for children. We shall more exactly, and less haphazardly, perceive the reason why these particular picture books are of the company that little children reach for instinctively and recall, in adult years, with eager clarity and affection.

The more sensitive our perception, the more nearly we shall be able to see the pictures and stories as a child sees them—with sympathetic concern and with joyous wonder and laughter. We will see too what the artist's own expression of his idea has to give to children—of beauty, truth, and imagination.

One of the importations from the Continent that has held its assured place with more than one generation of children is Jean de Brunhoff's

The Story of Babar. Listen to the singing rhythmic simplicity of the writing of Babar's story:

> In the Great Forest a little elephant was born. His name was Babar. His mother loved him dearly and used to rock him to sleep with her trunk, singing to him softly the while.[1]

The story has a French orderly and logical progression and is told with a judicious and witty minimum of words.

The novelty of the idea and the freshness with which Jean de Brunhoff develops the theme compels a child's interest. The affable charm of Babar's character makes him his friend. The impossible and absurd adjustments to city life which the little elephant undertakes with imperturbable poise are taken in faith by little children. In imagination they accompany him in his enjoyment of civilized amenities, as well as when he is at home in the Great Forest. Babar is given human characteristics as well as human clothing, yet he remains essentially an elephant, and after his brief excursion into human society, his instinctive return to his own kind is inevitable.

Jean de Brunhoff has drawn the pictures in bright, primary colors which contrast pleasurably with the elephant-gray of Babar and his elephant friends. The flat surface suggests a poster-like form which yet achieves a three-dimensional effect in the drawing of the characters so that we can see Babar advancing with the utmost naturalness into the life of the city. As we turn from one picture to another we become aware of the illustrator's care for the page itself, fitting the picture into it, alternating picture with text to produce a complementary balance. This balance reveals Brunhoff's feeling for over-all design—a superior quality in any picture book. In *The Story of Babar* there is a significant mingling of the real world and fantasia which suggests a libretto for a children's comic opera in the French mood.

Picture book illustrators are just as alive as other artists to what is taking place in the art world today. Their work is influenced by current trends. Present-day emphasis is on design, but we remember that design was not absent in the work of Walter Crane and Howard Pyle. Ludwig Bemelmans' picture book, *Madeline,* on the other hand, shows no recognizable design, perhaps because his intention is so obviously to jest with the child in a lighthearted pictorial manner, so close to what a child might do himself, that in this may lie the secret of the book's appeal to children. Bemelmans brings an exuberant

[1] Jean de Brunhoff, *The Story of Babar* (N.Y.: Random, 1933), p.1.

imagination, humor and subtlety to his vigorous drawings, whether in charcoal against a yellow background or in the rich color of the Tuileries Gardens in the sunshine.

Madeline pictures a little girl who does not for a moment stray out of a precise French pattern, yet who is universally within a child's knowledge. There is more than a hint of caricature in these drawings of children seen together in decorous straight rows indoors and out, and in the abandonment of conventional perspective in the pictures of Miss Clavel who "ran fast and faster." The sheer verve of the drawings carries the child along, although he may not always be aware of their subtle humor and caricature. He is caught by the exciting pitch of the action he sees in the detail of the pictures and hears in the rhyming verse in which the story is told. His perception and imagination cannot but absorb a little of the atmosphere of Paris, as well.

There could hardly be greater difference than we find in turning from *Madeline* to *The Story about Ping*, written by Marjorie Flack, with Kurt Wiese's illustrations. *The Story about Ping* has a simplicity innocent of caricature or elusive subtleties in story or pictures.

The collaboration of Marjorie Flack and Kurt Wiese is a happy one. Yet the question must arise in our minds whether Marjorie Flack's pictures for her own story might not have found an even happier expression than the interpretation of another artist. Marjorie Flack may not be one of the most distinguished of modern illustrators, yet her pictures of familiar family pets—dogs, cats, farmyard ducks and geese—have an intimate reality and a simple activity that entertain little children with their happy, instantaneous appeal. Children are fascinated by the vividness with which Marjorie Flack has caught the personality of a Scotch terrier puppy called Angus. Gay, heedless but sensitive to rebuke, he romps through the misadventures of the day in a series of episodes which have little discernible plot. The pictures are in bright bold masses of color, in which the decorative but unobtrusive background emphasizes the activity of the animal characters of the story.

In *The Story about Ping*, the story of a Chinese duck on the Yangtze River, Marjorie Flack shows a greater sense of both humor and plot than in her *Angus* books. The simplicity of her affectionate portrayal of Ping's adventures when he fails to return to the houseboat home captivates the sympathy of every child. Kurt Wiese's pictures for the story have an elementary truthfulness and an uncluttered directness that tie them closely to the text. He re-creates as a background the busy commerce of the Yangtze River with its one-eyed houseboats, curious woven baskets and ominous-looking cormorants. It is difficult to imagine that any other illustrator, even Marjorie Flack herself, could have more faithfully interpreted or more authentically pictured the scene and events of the story.

The unity of a picture book is evident when the story and the pictures carry us simultaneously to the dramatic climax of the story and then on to the denouement. Edward Ardizzone has achieved this unity to a marked degree, from both a child's and a critic's viewpoint, in his picture book *Little Tim and the Brave Sea Captain*. The pictures are a delight to the trained eye. They have an engaging sketchy looseness in the drawing and a range of fine color that portrays the changing moods of the sea. The fast-moving action, the sturdy figures of Tim and his seaman friends, and the tossing ships on a stormy sea are set before us with circumstantial detail which children never tire of exploring for some particular they may have missed.

The text is a tale of adventure on the high seas. Its essential plot is that of any story of shipwreck, but transposed here into an idiom that a little child can grasp. For him it holds tense drama, and for the time being he *is* Little Tim and shares all his adventures. Tim is a stowaway, he learns the hardships of a seaman's life, he is shipwrecked and finally his rescue by cable restores him to his family and friends. The harmony between text and pictures is complete in the mood of excitement conveyed by the simple, rhythmic and sustained telling of the story and in the rapid and vivid lines, washed with stimulating and harmonious color.

The dramatic quality in the illustrations of *Little Tim and the Brave Sea Captain* becomes a dynamic force in H. A. Rey's picture book *Curious George*. Their dramatic effect is gained by strong color, vividly seen action and irregular vignetting—the exciting appeal of dark colors boldly brushed on white paper. The block formation gives an impact to the illustrations which is instantaneous in its appeal. Anyone, child or adult, is captivated by the skill with which the agility of the monkey, George, is caught and shown against a background of familiar scenes of city life. Rey's sense of dynamic design is easily seen in his pictures of the predicaments caused by a monkey's curiosity. No one could miss it, for example, in the group of policemen overturning the desk in search of Curious George.

The story has a breathless pace. The simplicity and brevity of the telling is rhythmic and dramatic. The sentences have space and shape. When Curious George finds himself in jail for his thoughtless misdeeds, his escape is told in words carefully chosen for their speed, animation, and sound.

> The bed tipped up, the gaoler fell over, and, quick as lightning, George ran out through the open door. He hurried through the building and out on to the roof. How lucky he was a monkey! Out he walked along the telephone wires. Quickly and quietly over the guard's head, George walked away. He was free![2]

The tempo and drama of the story are accented in the illustrations so that they advance together as one. No wonder little children return to *Curious George* again and again, finding there a picture book of the kind they are looking for.

In considering these five picture books as examples of those which meet a little child's criterion of what a picture book should be, we observe that they have a number of things in common. The imaginative quality of the idea of each is fresh and original. They all have a true theme. The theme is developed through the action and conforms, though in simple form, to the requirements of any good story. That is, there is a recognizable plot which has a beginning, a middle, and an end. Each story is about one character, the hero, with whom a child can identify himself whether the hero is an elephant, a Chinese duck, a monkey or just a little boy or a little girl. While the subject matter is imaginative, even sometimes fantastic, it is in every case related to the familiar. The combination is one that rejoices little children. Yet along with the familiar, the difference of experience between the hero and the child who looks and listens gives him a sense of extensions beyond his own limited environment and lifts his horizons.

Well-drawn pictures add the strength of visual impression to the vicarious experience children gain from a story, and it is significant that the illustrations of these picture books are good art. It is not that children recognize the art of the drawings. In the picture books they have taken to their hearts it is the *living* quality of the pictures that is the secret of their unfailing charm. The illustrations are drawn with the artist's skill, but they are drawn as well from the artist's heart that remembers a child's way of seeing, feeling and enjoying a world that is to him new, wonderful, and unexplored.

[2] H. A. Rey, *Curious George* (Boston: Houghton, 1921), p.[37-39].

ASSOCIATIVE READING

CRANE, WALTER. An Artist's Reminiscences. Methuen, 1907.

LANE, MARGARET. The Tale of Beatrix Potter. Warne, 1946.

MAHONY, BERTHA E.; LATIMER, LOUISE P., and FOLMSBEE, BEULAH, comps. Illustrators of Children's Books, 1744-1945. Horn Book, 1947.

PITZ, HENRY C. A Treasury of American Book Illustration. American Studio Books, 1947.

SPIELMANN, M. H., and LAYARD, G. S. Kate Greenaway. A. & C. Black, 1905.

CHAPTER NINE

The writing of children's books is even more of a gamble, whether one is doing it for art's sake or the butcher's, than the writing of a novel. On the one hand they have the insistent competition of their fore-runners to meet, as novels have not; on the other hand, if once they join their competitors on equal terms, then they . . . will outlive many a better novel of the same season.

A. A. Milne,
Books for Children

STORIES

"I'm beastly bored," said Robert.

"Let's talk about the Psammead," said Anthea who generally tried to give the conversation a cheerful turn.

"What's the good of talking," said Cyril. "What I want is for something to happen . . ."

Jane finished the last of her home-lessons and shut the book . . .

"We've got the pleasure of memory," said she . . .

"I don't want to think about the pleasures of memory," said Cyril. "I want some more things to happen."

"We're very much luckier than any one else, as it is," said Jane. "Why, no one else ever found a Psammead. We ought to be grateful."

"Why shouldn't we go on being, though?" Cyril asked, "—lucky, I mean; not grateful. Why's it all got to stop?"

"Perhaps something will happen," said Anthea, comfortably. "Do you know, sometimes I think we are the sort of people that things do happen to."

"It's like that in history," said Jane: "some kings are full of interesting things, and others—nothing ever happens to them, except their being born and crowned and buried, and sometimes not that."

"I think Panther's right," said Cyril. "I think we are the sort of people things do happen to. I have a sort of feeling things would happen right enough if we could only give them a shove. It just wants something to start it. That's all."[1]

Here, plainly stated, in the opening of E. Nesbit's story, "The Phoenix and the Carpet," is the *sine qua non* of a story for children—the writer must be able to give his story the "shove" which will start things happening. Otherwise there will be no story worth the name. The

[1] E. Nesbit, "The Phoenix and the Carpet" from *The Five Children*, reprinted by permission of Coward-McCann, Inc.

131

things that happen may be set in the past, the present or the future. They may happen in the everyday world or in the world of imagination. But however that may be, the characters of the story must be "the sort of people things do happen to" if the story is to hold the interest of its restless and active audience.

In other words, the immediate allure of a story for children is in what happens. Where it happens, and to whom, are only there, to a child, because events must happen somewhere and to someone. Place, time, and characters are necessary for the sake of the story, to give it actuality and to increase the pleasure it gives. How and why things happen in a story are seldom analyzed by a child, but in these lie the skill of a writer in luring the reader on to find out "what happens next," in creating an atmosphere in the story of surprise and suspense. If a child does not care what is about to happen, there is no story, and the only reaction that is felt is disappointment.

Children do genuinely and unblushingly read "for pleasure" and if they do not find it they make no pretense of enjoyment. But pleasure is a relative term, capable of infinite variety and interpretation. A child's enjoyment of one story differs in kind and degree from his enjoyment of another. The measure of his pleasure in a book is not solely the immediate attraction of its exciting events. That this is so can be seen from those stories which a child reads again and again, seeming to find in them an inexhaustible pleasure beyond the mere events of a story which is already familiar to him. If suspense and surprise are all the story has to offer and if "what happens next" is the single attraction the book affords, a second reading must lose all the excitement of the first. Let us examine, if we can, the elements that, taken together, give an experience of pleasure that goes beyond the moment and is repeated with each re-reading.

The test of fiction, whether for adults or for children, is the quality of the experience we receive in reading it. This quality depends upon the writer's conception of his subject, upon his treatment of it, and upon the expression he gives to it. The idea may be trivial but the treatment of it gay and beguiling. In another book the idea may have significance but the expression of it be inadequate or dull. On the other hand, a writer's idea, treatment, and expression may communicate a unified and coherent experience which has truth and significance for the reader. Since we may assume that a writer writes as well as he can, the quality of the experience his book can give the reader is the test of the writer himself. No book can give an experience which it is not in its writer to give, and the quality of the experience depends also upon the feeling and judgment of the reader, upon his ability to apprehend and appreciate.

Children's reactions to the stories they read are as personal as those of adults. There are no books that "all children like" any more than there are novels that all adults enjoy. But there are stories which all children should be given an opportunity to like if they are not to miss the unique experience which is the greatest pleasure a good book can give; the kind of reading experience to which children return again and again as to an unfailing spring of clear water.

The years of childhood are the years of wonder and question and surmise. A child's active and ranging mind can find in books, and nowhere so well as in good books, the material to enrich the experiences of these years, in spite of the limited and uneventful environment which is the usual lot of childhood. The quality of the material children find in books is fundamentally important. Although children have strong individual likes and dislikes, they are uncritical in the sense that their literary judgments have only the validity of their years and inexperience. They have not as yet progressed to the point of reasoning and analysis. Unfortunately, too, in the case of inferior stories, children bring so much of their own imagination and concentration to the reading of a book that even the commonplace book is enhanced for them by their own racing fancy.

Many adults have had this experience in childhood. The danger is that adults, relatively unconscious of having progressed in their literary judgments, do not discard the memory of a book which once, as children, they found pleasure in. If childish memories take the place of later judgment and revaluation, they can perpetuate the continued reading of a sentimentalized or sensational or even merely commonplace book.

The argument has been used that a certain amount of mediocre reading does not hurt children: that adults also read, with pleasure and a kind of satisfaction, much that is not of first water, even those adults who are called intelligent readers. I think the analogy is a mistaken one. After all, adults remain adults for a long time and the span is lengthy enough to admit of some waste of time. In the case of children whose youthful and formative years are so brief, there is little time to waste. In childhood one is responsive and susceptible to influences to a greater degree, for better or for worse, than at any other period of life. When the possibilities and potentialities are unlimited—in spite of differences in the native intelligence of children—why give a child less than he can recognize and value, enjoy and make use of in his impulse toward growth?

As is true in the field of adult fiction, there are children's stories which claim our serious consideration and there are others which do not. There are stories of which the reading of a few pages only will reveal a hackneyed idea, a threadbare plot, and trite situations, expressed in commonplace language. It is not difficult to recognize an inferior book which has no good points to recommend it to our attention. The real test of critical judgment is the evaluation of those books which in greater or less degree have a right to serious criticism. A fair and reasoned appraisal of current children's fiction is most difficult of all, for these books are untested by time. Any claim we make for them as to permanent value must be determined in the future, not in the present. But it is here among current books, where the difficulty of judging rightly is greatest, that the necessity for understanding the underlying principles of creative fiction is most important.

These underlying principles cannot be stated as a set of rules to be learned and applied to any new book we may read. The recognition of literature is never automatic. It can be acquired, however, through analysis of those stories which have given pleasure to successive generations of children, stories which are acknowledged to be literature and which have initiated new phases in the history of children's books. Our faith in our judgment of new books must rest in whatever qualities they possess in common with those books whose hold on the children remains constant and whose experience of pleasure is of the kind to which children return with fresh delight.

Such stories as *Robinson Crusoe, Alice in Wonderland, Treasure Island, Sir Nigel, The Jungle Book, Tom Sawyer* and *Huckleberry Finn* have each in its own way extended and enriched the field of writing for children. They have initiated the three chief divisions or classes of children's stories which may roughly be called fantasy, historical fiction, and stories of actuality. All three classes have great range and flexibility. All can and indeed should be adventure stories, and their borders sometimes touch. Fantasy and historical fiction have their special requirements, in addition to those of a good story, and will be dealt with in succeeding chapters. Our concern now is with the fiction of actuality. These stories may range from those which are entirely within a child's experience to those which give children an experience outside their limited environment, but which they can enjoy, vicariously, and so gain the enhancement of life they are seeking in the hazards of more adventurous lives.

"Stories of actuality" is not a winning name for a kind of reading to which children turn in expectation of high adventure and romance—adventure which *might* be true. In a speech given to the Royal Society of Literature, Kipling said, "For fiction is Truth's elder sister. Obviously! No one in the world knew what truth was till someone had told a story." In a story which might happen, when the events are purely imaginary but nevertheless appear plausible and possible, the story is true to some aspect of life. Such adventures provide the vicarious experience which widens children's interests, lifts their horizons, and satisfies their need for an imaginative outlet.

In all the range of that class of fiction which, ostensibly at least, deals with stories of real life, those of high adventure are most universal in interest. They are also, as a rule, simple and straightforward and lend themselves to analysis. Most of them are the outcome of what might be called the high spirits of their writers. Their aim, usually, is simply to spin a good yarn, to write an adventure tale often with a seasoning of pirates, treasure hunting, or smuggling. The flavor of the sea pervades many of the best adventure stories.

The sea, especially to children, carries with it the spell of the unknown and unexplored, of wonders untold. And since the sea is not man's natural element, it carries also the implication of ships and the hazards of fire, mutiny, or shipwreck. The isolation of a ship has almost the fascination of a desert island and in emergencies brings out Crusoe-like qualities of courage, ingenuity, energy, and enterprise. Evil men find the sea a fine concealer of crime. The limited boundaries of a ship and the restrictions they impose can be the cause of turbulent and conflicting emotions. The whole subject lends itself to romance.

It is true that most, if not all, of the stories that are called sea adventure have a great preoccupation with other matters. If we think of the favorite stories whose background is the sea we find that *Treasure Island* is really a pirate story, *Twenty Thousand Leagues Under the Sea* purports to reveal scientific discovery, *Captains Courageous* tells of fishing off the Grand Banks, *Jim Davis* is a story of smuggling, and *The Dark Frigate* deals with the slave trade. But whatever aspect of the subject these books may take, the tang of salt water has a pervasive influence.

When Robert Louis Stevenson blazed a new trail with his story of *Treasure Island* he not only wrote a great pirate story, he also influenced much subsequent writing for children, giving it a trend toward an ever widening field of high adventure. Many writers who followed in this field failed to grasp the important fact that it is not alone the *adventure* of *Treasure Island* that has made it so beloved by children. Its inherent qualities are those of a writer whose creative imagination is joined with a masterly prose style, an association which has given the book its staying power.

Let us see what an analysis of *Treasure Island* will reveal. The story is told in the first person by Jim Hawkins, a boy whom chance involves in a strange adventure. By the device of the first person Stevenson gives his story a plausibility, an appearance of truth necessary to all romance. It also gives a consistent and unified point of view—Jim's— which throws the events into sharper relief. Jim himself reports his experience. It fills his memory with strong and vivid pictures full of color. Who could resist the first one he describes at the beginning of the book:

> I remember him as if it were yesterday, as he came plodding to the inn door, his sea chest following behind him in a hand-barrow; a tall, strong, heavy, nut-brown man; his tarry pigtail falling over the shoulders of his soiled blue coat; his hands ragged and scarred, with black, broken nails; and the sabre cut across one cheek, a dirty, livid white. I remember him looking round the cove and whistling to himself as he did so, and then breaking out in that old sea-song that he sang so often afterward:
>
> > Fifteen men on the dead man's chest—
> > Yo-ho-ho, and a bottle of rum!
>
> in the high, old tottering voice that seemed to have been tuned and broken at the capstan bars. Then he rapped on the door. . .

Jim himself is not a memorable character, although he has substance enough to be credible. There is no need for more. He is there to tell the story. Because he sees it as a boy would see it, a child can identify himself with Jim, live through the stirring scenes he describes, and come to know the strange company aboard the "Hispaniola." The story itself is not a mere string of exciting events. Stevenson is a master at constructing plot and *Treasure Island* is one of his best. We not only know what happens, we know why it happens. The events move logically and inexorably to a climax. Although a child's interest, while reading *Treasure Island,* is mainly in the tense, swiftly moving narrative, it is the larger-than-life size characters of the story which live in his memory. Children like strong, colorful characters as much as adults do. In the smooth-tongued, ruthless pirate, Long John Silver, they meet a terrifying, yet somehow likeable buccaneer. His individuality grows in their minds until he takes on a reality that makes pirates in other books seem mere pieces of stage property in comparison. The characters in many pirate stories seem unreal because while they are shown in action, the reader has no clue to the motivation which governs their conduct and actions. The events of the story, while they may be dramatic and exciting, seem to take place without regard to the kind of people involved. The reader has no way of getting inside the minds of the characters, no way of knowing them as he comes to know Long John Silver, because the author is writing about his characters from the outside and sees them only as stage properties necessary to carry the action of the story.

This is not Stevenson's method. The reader comes to know the characters not only through their own revealing speech, but by direct and indirect hints and suggestions. The characters come alive for the reader because he knows *how* they think and what effect this has on events. Nothing happens that is not related to the individuality of the characters.

And how simple, vigorous, and eloquent is the telling of the story of *Treasure Island;* the apt, unusual word, the pictorial phrase, the striking similes which effectively suggest a picture to the imagination. The story is so fresh, brushed in with such sure, suggestive strokes, that it is impressed on the reader as a concentrated essence of experience etched forever on the mind. No wonder it has passed into the permanent literature of childhood.

I have said that *Treasure Island* blazed a new trail in the field of adventure. In the history of children's literature it is evident that the influence, the impact of a very few books has changed and enlarged the whole field of writing for children. These books are recognized as important and original works of literature; they have initiated a new trend and have had a host of imitators. In the field of adventure, there are not only imitators, there are writers who have given a fresh and original direction to the adventure story.

The unreluctant years

When Arthur Ransome wrote *Swallows and Amazons* he originated a new kind of adventure story. The escape from the limited environment of the child's everyday, or even holiday life is obviously the writer's intention here, as it is in *Treasure Island*. But the adventure theme of *Swallows and Amazons* is woven into the fabric of the imaginative play of a child's mental world. Romance becomes not a distant unattainable prospect, but waits on the threshold of every child's imagination. Arthur Ransome, in all his writing, seems to be saying to his readers that one way to come alive and find life an exciting adventure is to open the door of imagination.

Whether Arthur Ransome writes of imaginative or actual adventure, his stories tell of boats and water-ways where he is entirely at home. His serious purpose in writing his books can be seen not only in their solid content but also in his themes. The theme of *Great Northern?* for instance, is developed with such skill and sympathy that it calls for serious study and analysis.

Arthur Ransome has a concern for the wild birds that nest in river sedge or on shores of lonely lakes near the sea. In more than one of his stories he makes this concern not his alone, but that of his imagined characters. Since children tend to identify themselves with the characters of their stories, the result is that concern for wild life is carried over and becomes as operative in the reading child as it is in the imagined characters, one of whom exclaims "This is better than anything that's happened yet. Three cheers for natural history. Great Auks and Guillemots! I never thought birds could be half such fun."

The idea at the back of *Great Northern?* is the protection of wild life, but this subject is an abstraction which the concrete minds of children find too diffuse to grasp in any broad sense. So Arthur Ransome has given his idea a particular aspect. The emphasis falls on the identity of the diving bird that Dick, the "ship's naturalist" discovers nesting in the Hebrides. Is it or isn't it a Great Northern?

The importance of a discovery which proves all existing bird books inaccurate now takes precedence and governs the action of the story. The individual characters realize the necessity of subordinating their conflicting desires and plans under a common compulsion—their obligation to genuine scientific discovery. Dick must be enabled to photograph the birds because, in the words of the villain of the piece, "what's hit's history, what's missed mystery." In other words, there must be proof.

138

This, in the main, is the idea behind the story. That it has real significance for children is undeniable. Whether it will hold their attention depends on the construction of the story and the way it is told. Let us look first at the framework.

Arthur Ransome is not a writer who overlooks the points which make a story a good one in the minds of his readers. He creates characters of the kind to whom things happen and he is skilful in giving the "shove" that starts them happening. Birds have enemies, sometimes human enemies, and to "confound their knavish tricks" provides the action and interaction of the book. The construction, with this basis, makes an interesting study in the working out of a plot. In a preliminary excursion inland from the cove where their boat is anchored, some of the children in the story explore the heather-covered uplands while Dick with his passion for birds follows the shore line of two small lochs in the hope of adding to the list of birds seen on the voyage. Dick discovers the Great Northern Divers nesting on a small island and makes a quick sketch, uncertain of their identity. The others find their movements are being watched by unfriendly inhabitants—that they are, in fact, being stalked.

On their return to the ship Dick is puzzled to discover that while his drawing corresponds with the picture of the Great Northern in his bird guide, the book states clearly that these birds "nest abroad." Yet he had seen them nesting here. Their ship returns to the harbor and the cruise is over, or so they all think. But Dick finds a "bird man" whose ship is in the harbor and visits him to get his opinion on the identity of the Diver. To Dick's horror the bird man is in reality an enemy of birds who shoots and stuffs them and collects their eggs for his private collection. His interest in Dick's discovery convinces the others of its scientific importance.

The conviction that Dick's birds are in danger of extermination, the need to circumvent the bird man's cruel design, and the importance of photographing the discovery are now of paramount importance to the characters of the story. Their ship returns to the cove where the discovery was made. At this point the pattern of the story is woven of three threads: Dick stalks the birds, the natives stalk the children, and the villain stalks Dick. All three threads converge at the point where the original discovery was made; the climax is dramatic and the conclusion follows with dispatch.

We see that, so far, the story has significance and a well-constructed plot in which suspense is built up to a dramatic climax. But to suggest that in these lie the reason for the lasting pleasure Arthur Ransome's stories have for children would be to ignore the qualities which constitute his right to stand beside the other writers of permanent books of children's literature. The fusion of his storytelling genius with his art as a writer marks his stature as a creative writer. In *Great Northern?* we can discern three distinct styles of writing, each appropriate to the matter in hand. Let us examine them.

Arthur Ransome is aware that most children are Robinson Crusoes at heart. They build rafts, construct all kinds of hiding places and explore underground as well as aboveground when they can. When he describes in careful detail how a ship is put on legs for "scrubbing," or the construction of a "picthouse," or the making of a "hide" behind which bird-watching may be carried on, Ransome is dealing with fundamental and universal interests of children and he writes about them with the precise minuteness and practical language of Defoe when he describes Robinson Crusoe's ingenious contrivances.

The dialogue, of which there is a great deal, is a device for advancing the story and realizing the characters. His style here is natural, lively, and unassuming. For instance, there is a council of war in the cabin after the ship returns to the cove: Nancy is summing up the situation in which they find themselves:

> "It's like this," she said. "There are two lots of enemies, not one. Dick's got to take his photographs without being seen by the old Dactyl. And he's got to do it without being seen by the natives. If the natives start yelling like they did at John and me, they'll frighten the birds and he won't have a chance."
>
> "It's worse than that," said Dick. "If the Gaels see me going to the island they'll start shouting, and that'll tell the egg-collector just where to look." He paused a moment as a new·thought came into his worried head. "Look here," he said. "There's something else. If the natives see what I'm doing, the egg-collector's only got to wait till we've gone. Then he'll ask them. They'll take his money and show him where the nest is and we won't be able to do anything about it."
>
> "Great Auks for ever!" exclaimed Nancy. "Well done, Professor. Of course that's what we'll do. We've got to use one lot of enemies against the other. Simple. We've got to find a way of making those Gaels do all their shouting in the wrong place."
>
> "But if they see me."

"They mustn't," said Nancy, "and they shan't. Look here, Titty. About that stalking the other day. Let's hear exactly what happened."

After hearing all about the adventure Nancy makes up her mind:

"What we've got to do," said Nancy, "is to get them stalking again."

"We don't want trouble with natives," said Captain Flint. "What sort of people are they?"

"There's a young chieftain," said Dorothea.

"And a huge old giant with a grey beard," said Titty.

"You saw him yourself," said Roger. "The dogmudgeon who wouldn't wave back when we waved to him as we sailed away."

"And there were others," said Dorothea. "All savage Gaels shouting Gaelic war cries on their native hills."[2]

Easy and colloquial as the dialogue is, it nevertheless reveals the individuality of each speaker. We know not only what the characters of his stories are doing at the moment, we know how they will be likely to act in any given situation. They are so well realized that they take on the attribute of actuality. To their readers the characters created by Arthur Ransome are often more real than many of their companions in everyday life.

As well as these two styles of writing—the practical and the conversational—Arthur Ransome has another way of writing, a way that is so subtly a part of the story that it creates imperceptibly a picture of beauty and meaning. For it is the Hebrides themselves that Arthur Ransome has written into his story of *Great Northern?*—the rocky coasts where gulls whirl and scream, the narrow coves, the heather growing on the hillsides, the mist-filled valleys where deer are grazing, the reed-bordered lochs where Dick heard for the first time the long wavering note "like wild laughter"—the cry of the Great Northern Diver.

We have seen that while good adventure stories are so constructed that the reader is carried along by excitement, danger, and suspense, there must be other factors present if the story is to give lasting pleasure or stand the test of re-reading. Characterization, atmosphere, significance, and narrative skill are factors which give permanence to a good story, distinct from thrills alone. These factors add, as well, to the reader's pleasure in his enjoyment of stories of a different kind

[2] Arthur Ransome, *Great Northern?* (N.Y.: Macmillan, 1947), p.212-13.

141

of actuality; those in which plot is of less importance than it is in the adventure story.

The stories which are intimately linked with children's everyday life, which reflect a child's own world, can have meaning and significance for the reader in the hands of a gifted writer. On the other hand the limited surroundings of children can make a book of this kind merely stereotyped and dull, or overdrawn and insincere. Children enjoy the matter-of-fact, down-to-earth detail of the everyday life of Robinson Crusoe. But his story is, of course, one of extraordinary adventure written about in an ordinary way, a quite different thing from ordinary life. Dealing with the latter, the writer's problem is to write a story well within the bounds of possibility, which yet invests the seeming matter-of-factness of everyday life with special interest and romance.

Stories of everyday life are commonly of more interest to the children of their day than to later generations of children. Few of them gain a permanent place among the books which survive. The reason for this is that they are, perforce, fitted into the framework of their time, its social life, manners, and attitudes. As their particular era recedes further and further into the past, the convention the children of the story live within recedes into the background and the story loses more and more of its significance and interest for later generations of child readers.

Those which survive must possess some special quality to lift them above the usual fate of their contemporaries, so that they outlive many of the popular books of their time. When we think of such books as *Six to Sixteen, The Treasure Seekers, Little Women, Tom Sawyer* and *Huckleberry Finn* it becomes clear that while they each in their different manner reflect the life of their times, they have in common a universality through which they compete on equal terms with books of the present. The writers of these books, we realize, are vividly remembering their own childhood, and bringing their later experience of life to illuminate the experience of childhood in its universal aspect.

In fiction concerned with everyday life, whether written for adults or children, the reader's interest commonly centers in the characters. If, as he reads, they take on color, movement, feeling, point of view, he is apt to say they are "true to life." When characters in stories for children have lifelikeness, they are not readily forgotten even though their way of life, their time, and place become more and more remote.

If we think of Jo March, Tom Sawyer, and Huck Finn, it is impossible not to realize that characters in contemporary stories will have difficulty in competing with characters of such color, vividness, and truth. Where they compete successfully, they, too, will survive beyond their own generation, for children are loyal to the heroes and heroines of their story books whose experience of life has meaning and truth for them.

Stories that are written within the convention of the writer's own time can mirror faithfully some aspect of that age, and so, with the passage of time, have value as social history. For example, apart from their literary art, the novels of Jane Austen have come to interpret and reconstruct for her readers the social convention of her times. What Jane Austen did for the drawing-rooms and ball-rooms of the nineteenth century adult, Mrs. Ewing has done for the school-rooms and play-rooms, the fields and gardens of the nineteenth century child.

Like Jane Austen Mrs. Ewing writes of people whose lives are far from great events. Her stories have no real plot, no great depth of character drawing, no stirring events. They are a minute and leisurely treatment of the everyday external life of the children of her day. But, as Jane Austen refuses to go beneath the surface of her characters' words and actions, so Mrs. Ewing refrains from making problems of her child characters' minds. At the same time no one sees small, insignificant things through a child's eyes more truly and shrewdly than Mrs. Ewing.

She sees what might be termed their "worldly vanities," their small embarrassments and mortifications, as well as their pleasures and triumphs. The incidents she relates are told in such a way that the utmost effect is gained from the minimum of action. Mrs. Ewing was a product of her time and although, like Jane Austen, she amuses her readers with the oddities and foibles of her characters, she does introduce a serious paragraph now and then. But lest any moral teaching should prove tedious it is inevitably lightened by humor, as for instance in this revealing episode from *Mary's Meadow:*

> I remember once Mother had been trying to make us forgive each other's trespasses, and Arthur would say that you cannot *make* yourself feel kindly to them that trespass against you; and Mother said if you make yourself do right, then at last you get to feel right; and it was very soon after this that Harry and Christopher quarrelled, and would not forgive each other's trespasses in the least, in spite of all that I could do to try and make peace between them.
>
> Chris went off in the sulks, but after a long time I came upon him

in the toy-cupboard, looking rather pale and very large-headed, and winding up his new American top, and talking to himself.

When he talks to himself he mutters, so I could only just hear what he was saying, and he said it over and over again:

"Dos first and feels afterwards."

"What are you doing, Chris?" I asked.

"I'm getting ready my new top to give to Harry. Dos first feels afterwards."

"Well," I said, "Christopher, you *are* a good boy."

"I should like to punch his head," said Chris—and he said it in just the same sing-song tone—"but I'm getting the top ready. Dos first and feels afterwards."

And he went on winding and muttering.

Mrs. Ewing's stories are not universal books in the sense that they have a popular appeal. They are more likely to be read by children who are capable of appreciating the less obvious in character delineation, atmosphere, and writing, perhaps the kind of children who later in life will turn to Jane Austen and other writers of novels of manners.

In these simple and graceful journals of commonplace happenings is found the quality that has given them permanence. For, while the experience of life here is different from that of children today, the characters of these stories are created out of the eternal stuff of childhood, and their naturalness and truth are valid in any age.

E. Nesbit's stories for children, like Mrs. Ewing's books, have their setting within the convention of a period which is gradually receding into the past. But the reversion the reader must make is negligible, for E. Nesbit did not write miniature novels of manners. The social convention in which her characters live is only incidental. The resemblance to any family group of children makes it easy for a child reading one of her stories to fancy himself one of them, not mentioned by the author, but able to take part in each adventure. For it is E. Nesbit's quality that she has invested the everyday life of children with special possibilities—with romance. She has also the faculty of projecting her readers into the imaginative minds of her characters so that identification with them is swift and effortless.

In her story of *The Treasure Seekers,* E. Nesbit's theme is not an unfamiliar one. Six motherless children, whose father's business has fallen on evil days, make plans to restore the fortunes of their house. Their projects include looking for buried treasure, being detectives, and editing a magazine. Each scheme not only draws the reader on to see how that particular situation is resolved but carries him along to "what next." In the building up of suspense E. Nesbit has a sure hand. As each unsuccessful project is abandoned, the reader is full of hope that the resourcefulness of the children will eventually be rewarded with success, but the issue remains in doubt until the climax because so many promising avenues turn out to be dead ends.

While the plot fulfils its purpose of arousing interest and creating suspense, it is also used as a means of developing characters who live in reality. The individuality of E. Nesbit's children is demonstrated in their delightful talk, so real, natural, and spontaneous that it is possible to think of the characters as people without benefit of author. In *The Treasure Seekers,* the first book of the Bastable saga, the characters are seen from the point of view of Oswald Bastable, a young boy whose spirit of enterprise and adventure is colored, like Tom Sawyer's, by his reading. Oswald Bastable tells of the wholehearted manner with which he and his brothers and sisters throw themselves into their projects. In their enthusiasm they do not always foresee the result of their well intentioned ideas.

The humor, so present in E. Nesbit's stories, proceeds from the contrast between the large ideas of the children and the ludicrous situations that develop as a consequence. The humor is also in the manner of writing; in the contrast between Oswald's grave, straightforward accounts and his lapses into a grandiloquent style composed of all the phrases he has found in his reading. These stories, full of action, of humor, and of character, are written from inside the minds of children. Each character is equally childlike and believable and moves through these lively and original stories as convincingly today as when the books were written. They are the universal child, and so are timeless.

The family chronicle of *Little Women,* since its appearance in 1868, has probably reached a larger public than any family story written for children. Its sustained popularity over generations confirms that in Jo March, Louisa Alcott has created the universal girl, as Mark Twain, in Tom Sawyer, shows the universal boy. But it seems clear, as well, that the reading of *Little Women* leaves the reader with a sense of the universality of family life that gives impact and reality and verisimilitude to the story.

Like Mrs. Ewing's stories, *Little Women* has no plot. The structure of events has no suspense rising to a climax. It relies for its interest on the reader's concern for the characters of the story. The everyday happenings are those of fairly uneventful lives, but they are implicit in the characters and so take on lifelikeness and reality as family experience—an experience in which humor and pathos are interwoven as they are in life, then and now.

In its nineteenth century New England setting, the story of *Little Women* has gradually acquired the significance of social history. Like Mrs. Ewing's stories, it reflects truthfully the memory of childhood and girlhood in an age whose social convention grows more and more remote from the reader. But to the child readers, the emotional identification which they make with the characters illuminates the pages of a story whose freshness and vitality is re-affirmed for each succeeding generation.

When we think of stories, written within the convention of the author's own time and place, which still continue to live in the minds and hearts of later generations of children, the books that come foremost to mind are *Tom Sawyer* and *Huckleberry Finn*. We can test the truth of this assumption by simply creating mental pictures of Tom and Huck, and then compare these with other characters in stories. Which has the greater vividness and color for us?

Although *Tom Sawyer* and *Huckleberry Finn,* with their setting of the semi-frontier, semi-nomadic life of Mark Twain's boyhood near, and on, the Mississippi have now a value as social history, it is not as history that these books continue to captivate children. When children return again and again to *Tom Sawyer* and *Huckleberry Finn* they are drawn by the adventure and fun which they are certain to find in the companionship of Tom, Huck and Jim. These are characters who have a continuing reality for the reader so that they go on living in the memory long after the book is read.

Perhaps not the least of the rewards of reading *Tom Sawyer* is that we are introduced in its pages to Huck, whose later adventures are recorded in *Huckleberry Finn.* Although there is little recognizable plot in this story, there is no lack of suspense. Huck's voyage down the Mississippi on a raft is a single, prolonged hazard for the reason that Huck's companion on the raft is Jim, a runaway negro slave. Every contact with people intensifies the danger of discovery and recapture.

The pattern of the book is woven from contrasting threads; the

146

contrast between the isolation of life on the raft and of Huck's expeditions to the various settlements ashore; the contrast between the exaggerated eccentricities of the "King" or the "Duke" and Huck's normal everyday nature; the contrast between the simple workings of Jim's mind and the complexity of Huck's conflicting loyalties. Mark Twain has given Huck not one, but two consciences. One of them has been superimposed on the other by the social convention of the time and place; a convention which requires Huck to regard a runaway slave as property he is bound to return to the owner. The other conscience is Huck's own. It is the voice of his loyal, human, pitying heart which cannot betray a friend who trusts in him.

Huck tells his story in the fluent, colloquial talk of an observant, but casually educated, boy whose spirit is in harmony with the rhythmically flowing river on which he is content to drift. The beauty, loneliness, and music of his river are echoed in Huck's words when he records his thoughts and feelings in the night watches:

> Not a sound anywhere—perfectly still—just like the whole world was asleep, only sometimes the bullfrogs a-cluttering, maybe. The first thing to see, looking away over the water, was a kind of dull line—that was the woods on t'other side; you couldn't make nothing else out; then a pale place in the sky; then more paleness spreading around; then the river softened up away off, and warn't black any more, but gray; you could see little dark spots drifting along ever so far away—trading-scows, and such things; and long black streaks —rafts; sometimes you could hear a sweep screaking; or jumbled-up voices, it was so still, and sounds come so far; and by and by you could see a streak on the water which you know by the look of the streak that there's a snag there in a swift current which breaks on it and makes that streak look that way; and you see the mist curl up off of the water, and the east reddens up, and the river . . . then the nice breeze springs up, and comes fanning you from over there, so cool and fresh and sweet to smell on account of the woods and the flowers; but sometimes not that way, because they've left dead fish laying around, gars and such, and they do get pretty rank; and next you've got the full day, and everything smiling in the sun, and the song-birds just going it!

The interweaving pattern of the story, its variety and color, so absorb the reader's fascinated interest that he is unaware of the lack of an apparent plot. When there is no logical progression from a beginning to a climax, and then to a denouement, the author must end his story in thc best way he can. The device that Mark Twain uses to bring the book to a conclusion is the almost unbelievable coincidence that Huck's aimless wanderings lead him to the door of Tom Sawyer's aunt. Incredible it may be, yet such a use of coincidence does not diminish our sense of the intuitive truth of the story of *Huckleberry Finn.*

It is only once in a long while that a book written for adult readers is taken over by children, and holds, like *Robinson Crusoe,* an enduring place in literature for children. Such books are always creative literature. Should not this fact suggest to us that our approach to children's books should place emphasis first of all on the creative quality their writers possess? Familiarity with those stories which are acknowledged to have this quality—a familiarity that is not casual, but both perceptive and critical—is essential for anyone concerned with the appraisal of children's books and the guidance of children's reading. Such familiarity will give a sense of perspective and proportion, will ensure the possession of guiding values, values which attend the recognition of a creative quality in a story for children.

ASSOCIATIVE READING

BENTLEY, PHYLLIS ELEANOR. Some Observations on the Art of Narrative. Macmillan, 1947. Home & Van Thal, 1946.

CATHER, WILLA. On Writing; Critical Studies on Writing As an Art. Knopf, 1949.

FORSTER, E. M. Aspects of the Novel. Harcourt, Brace, 1927. Edward Arnold, 1927.

MONTAGUE, C. E. A Writer's Notes on His Trade, with an introductory essay by H. M. Tomlinson. Doubleday, Doran, 1930. Chatto & Windus, 1930.

TREASE, GEOFFREY. Tales Out of School. Heinemann, 1948.

WHARTON, EDITH N. The Writing of Fiction. Scribner, 1925.

WOOLF, VIRGINIA. Mr. Brown and Mrs. Bennett (in *The Captain's Death Bed and Other Essays*). Harcourt, Brace, 1950. Hogarth Pr., 1950.

CHAPTER TEN

Your wife . . . can hardly, being a woman, dislike The Butterfly That Stamped. It is just possible, however, that she may remain indifferent to it as a trifle, a playing with fancies, of obvious purport, silly in its language, unworthy of attention. This simply means that she is educated above its knowledge, that she has outgrown it—in a word, that she is old.

Brian Hooker,
"Types of Fairy Tales"
in *The Forum*

FANTASY

 Like poetry, fantasy uses a metaphorical approach to the perception of universal truth. The word fantasy comes from the Greek, and, literally translated, means "a making visible." *The Shorter Oxford English Dictionary* defines fantasy as "the mental apprehension of an object of perception," and as "imagination; the process, the faculty, or the result of forming representations of things not actually present." That is to say, fantasy comes from the creative imagination, a power the mind has of forming concepts beyond those derived from external objects which are present to our senses.

There are factors other than imagination which determine the enduring place in literature of any book of fantasy, such as the writer's experience of life and his power of language, among others. But since he has chosen to write a book of fantasy, the degree of creative imagination he possesses must be our first concern. Creative imagination is more than mere invention. It is that power which creates, out of abstractions, life. It goes to the heart of the unseen, and puts that which is so mysteriously hidden from ordinary mortals into the clear light of their understanding, or at least of their partial understanding. It is more true, perhaps, of writers of fantasy than of any other writers except poets that they struggle with the inexpressible. According to their varying capacities, they are able to evoke ideas and clothe them in symbols, allegory, and dream.

The degree of a writer's capacities may range from the original and creative expression of a Lewis Carroll or the other-worldly vision of a George Macdonald, down to the merely invented or manufactured story which their authors mistake for genuine fantasy. A long series of fantastic happenings which are unrelated (except that some of the same characters reappear) and which follow no logical course of development and arrive nowhere, makes tedious reading. When we find that a book of so-called fantasy is full of trite phrases, pretty-pretty sentiments, and contrived rather than imagined events, and when the writing is forced and condescending, the result is not fantasy but shoddiness and fatuity. This leads us to conclude that writers who are inexpert, or who are unaware of the rare qualities required for genuine fantasy should avoid attempting to write it.

Every book of fantasy cannot be an *Alice in Wonderland,* but if it is to be given serious consideration as literature it must contain some of the ingredients found in *Alice* and in all good fantasies. There are certain well-written books of fantasy which give a genuine if simple kind of pleasure, whose values are those of entertainment and lively humor. There is undeniable enjoyment in A. A. Milne's imaginative insight into the private lives of toy animals, in the combination of unexpectedness and moral rectitude in Mary Poppins, in the genial Doctor Dolittle's preference for the company of animals, in the predicaments of the Doll family shipwrecked on Floating Island, in the resourceful enterprise of Mr. Popper and his penguins. Such books have their own integrity and value, though these are perhaps too weighty words with which to burden their gaiety, simplicity, and charm, or to describe their quality.

There are other books of fantasy that are less simple in their content and in the intention of their authors. As a painting has lights and shadows, perspective, and a richness of depth that leads us on further and further into the picture, these books grow in significance the longer we ponder over them. If we look at Rumer Godden's story of *The Dolls' House,* for instance, there is much to delight us as it is, on its face value: the miniature scale of domestic activity, the perfection of detail, the drama of the story. We can look further into it, as into a picture, and enjoy it also as a period piece, with its Victorian atmosphere and its well-grounded setting in London. But if we see no more than that, enjoyable as it is, we miss the quality that sets *The Dolls' House* apart from other doll and toy fantasies.

This book reaches out beyond its doll characters into the fundamental questions of human life: good and bad; right and wrong; the recognition of true as opposed to ephemeral values. These are questions that are universally important. They are themes found in all great literature. To find them treated in this microscopic way does not lessen their importance; perhaps it even clarifies them and brings them into perspective. It will be argued that this inner meaning eludes children and that their enjoyment of the book is solely in the story it tells. But perceptive children cannot help hearing some of these overtones and so becoming more sensitively aware of the world about them.

It is difficult to explain the distinction between true values and the lack of them in books of fantasy, but it is a distinction that is clearly recognized when they are present, and is even more noticeable in their absence. The ability to distinguish is gained by familiarity with great fantasy, by an understanding of the quality that sets it apart from other forms of fiction, although at the same time it must also be judged by the standards we apply to all fiction.

Fantasy, like other books of fiction, must first of all tell a story. It must arouse our interest and concern for the imagined characters whose story the author tells, whether they be human, supernatural beings, animals, or toys. It must show the characters in relation to each other and to the things that happen to them in a way to arouse our curiosity. The rising scale of suspense must ascend to the climax and the story round itself out with a satisfying inevitability. A book of fantasy must also conform to the standards of good writing which we apply to all fiction. But fantasy lives in a different climate from other fiction—in an atmosphere of reality in unreality, of credibility in incredibility.

The values of fantasy may be irrelevant to those of the fiction of actuality, yet they have their own laws and conventions to be accepted and understood if we are to approach the subject with a sound basis for critical judgment. A child's ready acceptance of fantasy is based on imagination and wonder. An adult lacking these universal attributes of childhood is often at a loss when he is asked to consider seriously a work of purely imaginative content, far removed from the reality of his experience of life. Before the adult can feel at ease in this different world of fantasy he must discover a means of approach. There is an interesting discussion on fantasy by E. M. Forster in his *Aspects of the Novel,* in which he says: "Our easiest approach to a definition of any aspect of fiction is always by considering the sort of demand it makes on the reader . . . what does fantasy ask of us? It asks us to pay something extra."[1]

That is to say that over and above what we ordinarily bring to the reading of a story, fantasy demands something extra, perhaps a kind of

[1] E. M. Forster, *Aspects of the Novel* (N.Y.: Harcourt, 1949), p.101.

sixth sense. All children have it, but most adults leave it behind with their cast-off childhood. There is a story from Kipling's *Puck of Pook's Hill* called "Dymchurch Flit," which suggests that this sixth sense was a gift of the fairies to their human friends. It tells that when Henry the Eighth set all England by the ears with his Reformation the fairies were driven to take refuge in Romney Marsh, crying "Fair or foul, we must flit out o' this, for Merry England's done with, an' we're reckoned among the Images."

The fairies packed into the marsh until it was filled with the heaviness of their wailing, and the trouble of it brought the Widow Whitgift one night to her door. At first she thought it was all the frogs in the dikes peeping. Then that it was the sound of the reeds. At last she heard the fairies cry to her to lend them her sons to man a boat so they could make their escape to France. When the boat left England, only Puck of all the little people remained behind; Puck—and the gift the grateful fairies promised the Widow Whitgift: that in every generation there would be one of her family who could see further through a stone wall than most.

This "something extra," this ability to see further through a stone wall than most, requires what many people are unwilling to give. It asks of the reader what Coleridge calls "the willing suspension of disbelief." The presence of fantasy in a story constitutes a barrier for many people. They think their intelligence incapable of accepting the premise of suspended reality. Yet in fantasy are found perhaps the most subtle and profound ideas in books written for children. All that is needed is a willingness to listen with sympathy to what the writer is saying. As in all other reading, if one has no desire to listen, no pleasure can result whatever the creative power of the writer or the intellectual content of the book.

Let us consider *Alice in Wonderland* as an example. Probably no other book of fantasy has paid such "dividends of pleasure" through childhood into maturity to those who have brought that "something extra" to the reading of Lewis Carroll. Yet there are people to whom the mention of *Alice* brings only vague memories of a little girl and a rabbit, or perhaps a mad hatter, or a Cheshire cat. Perhaps, as Percy Lubbock has suggested in reference to reading books of fiction, "our glimpse of it was too fleeting, it seems, to leave us with a lasting knowledge of its form." An inattentive or a cursory reading of *Alice in Wonderland* may indeed leave us with only a confused impression of fantastic happenings, as unrelated and formless as half-forgotten dreams. It is only when we give ourselves wholly to the book, allowing Lewis Carroll to have his way with us, that we find in *Alice* the quality of lasting pleasure so many other people have enjoyed; nor will it surprise us to find lines from *Alice* quoted so often both in life and in literature.

The child, Alice, is herself frequently confused when her logic, the logic of forthright common sense, is opposed by a totally different logic which seems fantastic to her, but against which no argument carries weight. When the White Queen says to her "The rule is, jam to-morrow and jam yesterday—but never jam *today*," Alice objects.

"It *must* come sometimes to 'jam today.' "

"No, it can't," said the Queen. "It's jam every *other* day: to-day isn't any *other* day, you know."

"I don't understand you," said Alice. "It's dreadfully confusing!"

But the reader is not confused. He appreciates the fantastic logic of the queen as well as he understands Alice's matter-of-fact point of view. Surely an early acquaintance with *Alice in Wonderland* should reduce the possibility of holding too many dogmatic opinions and increase a willingness to hear another person's point of view, fantastic though it may seem. However that may be, the book itself, the wit and imagination of Lewis Carroll are here for a second reading, if the first proved inauspicious.

When we analyze *Alice in Wonderland* we see that it is not, as *Pilgrim's Progress* or *Gulliver's Travels,* a thinly disguised allegory or a satire on life. It depends on other qualities for its unity. Lewis Carroll builds up striking patterns of language and idea, each part held in subtle relation to the others. The unity of the book is not in the design alone, but also in the consistent point of view. The story is Alice's dream as Alice dreamed it; the point of view is invariably that of the rational child in an irrational dream. The language is the language of nonsense, but at the same time we are sensible of the essence of truth it contains—for example, this dialogue during the trial concerning the theft of the tarts.

> "What do you know about this business?"
> "Nothing," said Alice.
> "Nothing *whatever?*" persisted the King.
> "Nothing whatever," said Alice.
> "That's very important," the King said, turning to the jury. They

were just beginning to write this down on their slates, when the White Rabbit interrupted:

"*Un*important, your Majesty means, of course," he said in a very respectful tone, but frowning and making faces at him as he spoke.

"*Un*important, of course, I meant," the King hastily said, and went on to himself in an undertone, "important—unimportant—unimportant—important—" as if he were trying which word sounded best.

Some of the jury wrote it down "important," and some "unimportant."

About this scene Paul Hazard says: "It is nonsense. But it is not pure invention: there are trials conducted in this way. We laugh for some profound reason of which we are hardly conscious, but which takes shape in our mind. The idea is caricatural, but it is not completely false. On the contrary it touches us by the element of truth that it contains."[2]

There are few incidents in the two *Alice* books which do not have what De la Mare calls "the compelling *inward* ring." Lewis Carroll may be joking when he upsets the accepted logic of events, but, as the Red Queen said to Alice, "even a joke should have some meaning." For instance: When Alice runs forward to meet the Red Queen whom she sees ahead of her she is bewildered to find that the Queen has disappeared. "*I* should advise you to walk the other way," said the Rose. This seemed nonsense to Alice but it was only when she did so that she found herself face to face with the Queen. Is there a suggestion here that what may appear nonsense can hold in its essence a higher truth not to be apprehended, perhaps, through the mere logic of common sense?

There are adults who have said that *Alice in Wonderland* is not a children's book. The implications of hidden meaning found on almost every page are not there for the child who reads the story. The brilliant and ironical wit the adult rejoices in is often not noticed by a child. It is said that when Lewis Carroll first told *Alice in Wonderland* on the river to three little girls, there was another auditor in the boat with them, an adult. He was a scholarly, perceptive, experienced colleague of Lewis Carroll's, who recognized the originality of the story and was urgent in having it written down.

[2] Paul Hazard, *Books, Children and Men* (Boston: Horn Book, 1944), p.140.

The unreluctant years

Perhaps these circumstances of the origin of the book give some clue to the right appreciation of it and to an understanding of the two levels of experience on which the book is written, and from which it must be approached and valued. To repeat Lewis Mumford's phrase "the words are for children and the meanings are for men." But it must not be forgotten that Lewis Carroll told Alice's adventures to entertain a little girl of seven who begged to have them written down so she could read them again and again. We remember too that when *Alice* was read aloud to six-year-old Greville, son of George Macdonald, he cried "There ought to be sixty thousand words of it!" *Alice in Wonderland* is a children's book as well as a universal one.

Little children enter freely and easily into the spirit of *Alice*. To them it is a story about a topsy-turvy world where anything can happen; where the Gryphon and the Mock Turtle went to school to learn Laughing and Grief (taught by an old crab) as well as the different branches of Arithmetic—"Ambition, Distraction, Uglification and Derision." To the children the story is full of good jokes and comical transpositions like these; to read it is a hilarious experience in which they identify themselves with Alice, the polite, trustful, yet curious child who follows a White Rabbit down a rabbit-hole and finds herself in a long lamp-lit hall with rows of locked doors. The tiny golden key she discovers fits a very little door through which she has a glimpse into "the loveliest garden you ever saw." But even her head was too large to go through the small door.

The plot of *Alice in Wonderland* revolves around Alice's determination to get into the enchanted garden, her efforts to do so being endlessly frustrated by the odd way things happen. "Curiouser and Curiouser" is how Alice expresses it. She is puzzled, too, to find that she doesn't keep the same size but is constantly changing, and it is not until she is the right size to go through the little door that she finds herself at last in the garden with the roses. It turns out that, besides roses, the garden has other, and less agreeable, inhabitants; that it is in fact the kingdom of the pack of cards. Alice's adventures among them flow faster and faster until she finds herself running hand in hand with the Gryphon to the final scene where the whole pack of cards collapses and Alice wakes up.

Both the *Alice* books are dream fantasies, the one built of a pack of cards, the other a game of chess. In each the illusion created by Lewis Carroll is so complete that we lose sight of the complicated and ingenious pattern of their structure. The books are undeniably written on two planes, that of the child and that of the adult. Perhaps it would be truer to say that the writing is a language to which the heart of childhood has the little golden key, while the implications of the ideas reveal themselves more and more with the added experience of life. As we ponder them we cannot wonder that *Alice in Wonderland* is to so many an inexhaustible source of pleasure in its crisp fresh humor, its rich and subtle symbolism, and the infinite speculation it leads to.

When we are considering the books of Lewis Carroll, it is impossible not to recall such writers of fantasy as Bunyan and Swift, Charles Kingsley and George Macdonald, W. H. Hudson and Kenneth Grahame. Various as these writers are in both gifts and methods, they have a common quality which makes their books memorable and universal. They are all men whose profound understanding and experience of life give significance to the creative ideas behind their writing. Each uses his own method and device. But since all are men of understanding, able to project their philosophy, their view of life, in the form of fantasy, their books have values over and above the story they tell. Their writing, too, is often touched with poetry.

Not all these authors wrote for children. It has happened in the past that a book written solely with adults in mind and with some adult concept to convey has been taken over by children and numbered among their classics. Such a book is *Pilgrim's Progress*, written by John Bunyan to inculcate in grown up sinners a sense of the burden of original sin they must carry throughout their earthly pilgrimage. But John Bunyan chose to clothe his theological teaching in rich allegory. He told it as an adventure story in simple and powerful language. Is it strange that children seized it for their own? Is it strange that children, who have followed with sympathy the fortunes of so many "younger sons" whose courage and endurance are tested in all the ways known to fairy tales, should find in Christian a similar, if more mysterious, hero beset as he is by difficulty and danger on his pilgrimage to the gates of the City of Light?

Bunyan had a moral purpose in writing *Pilgrim's Progress* but he saw and felt it as a human drama. This is the secret of the book's immortality. The story form in which it is told provides children with a fine adventure story which they like because it gives them a genuine experience of pleasure. And it gives more than that. The overtones of the writing suggest to the intuition of the child the spiritual world that he dimly apprehends and which, if he is a thoughtful child, he ponders in his attempts to understand the universe of which he is a part.

"How did the children happen to get hold of Swift?" asks Paul Hazard. Like *Pilgrim's Progress* and *Don Quixote, Gulliver's Travels* owes its place as one of the immortal classics of childhood to the fact that children stumbled on it in an age which produced little else from which children could obtain the imaginative sustenance they craved. *Gulliver's Travels* proved an antidote to the dreary moral and didactic tales with which their elders strove to improve the young.

Children have always refused to be bored by what does not interest them. They excel in the gentle art of skipping. It is the miniature world of Lilliputia and the reverse world of the giants that beguile them in *Gulliver's Travels.* As Paul Hazard says "They like its wild inventions that are not only comical but concrete." The rest of the book is forgotten.

A child's imagination is at times his *real* world. There is for him no abyss between the real and the unreal. He moves from the one to the other as he would move from one window to another. Like Lewis Carroll, Charles Kingsley and George Macdonald have used the dream fantasy when they wrote for children; but, unlike the author of *Alice,* these writers were preoccupied with the mysteries of the spiritual universe. They created a world of beauty and imagination in which a child is free to explain for himself the life of which he is a part.

George Macdonald has insight into the heart of a child. He understands the world that the child is seeking to discover; and he has the art of making these worlds of imagination much more real and vital than our everyday realm of facts and formulas. In *At the Back of the North Wind,* the North Wind is the personification of a child's questionings about things mortal and immortal. The reader is swept along as by a strange impelling force. The story answers for him the unanswerable; it gives him a vision of the mysterious and the inexplicable.

The story is about the boy Diamond, his relationship with his friend, North Wind, with his family, and with the people he meets along the way. It is a story with an underlying meaning as well, an underlying meaning declared as the tale unfolds. The story moves easily from the everyday world to the dream world by the simple device of having Diamond begin his travels in bed. That the bed is in a hayloft with only thin boards to keep out the wind and cold is reason enough for Diamond's sleep-walking and his dreams that are full of vague questionings.

George Macdonald gives expression to Diamond's inarticulate desires in his conversations with the North Wind during his dream journey. The conversations are presented with childlike simplicity and often with great beauty of expression. In this way, the child who reads Diamond's story is led to think about questions which are at the back of his mind, but which, being intangible, he cannot express.

The world of fantasy that George Macdonald creates is, for the time being, a real world which he presents as strange, magical, and mysterious. It is a believable world because the author's attitude is one of entire acceptance of its truth. The child who reads the book does not doubt that Diamond, child of the London street, can be whisked in a trice to the chill palaces of the North Wind.

The story, with its unpromising setting in a livery stable, deals with the commonplace happenings of the life of a little boy who through the power of imagination finds the realities of life, not in his everyday existence, but in the elemental world of the North Wind. The book begins in the hayloft, proceeds to Diamond's strange friendship with the North Wind, and reaches its climax with his experience at the back of the North Wind. The rest of the story tells what befalls when Diamond, with all his senses sharpened and aware, returns to everyday life.

Always true to the loyalties of human relationships, the story, even with its moralizing touches, still has room for nonsense and fun. Its basic structure is a childlike understanding of the fundamental principles of a way of life in which divine love and trust find wholehearted acceptance. As with all great books its inward spirit has something to say to each succeeding generation and to each individual child who keeps a heart open to wonder.

At the Back of the North Wind has a quality of pure imagination which, until it appeared, had been found only in the fairy tale. It is, perhaps, more didactic than one who read it in childhood remembers, but both qualities were part of the writer who was a Doctor of Divinity as well as an imaginative Scot.

The literature of fantasy is various, both in subject and treatment. It has, however, a tendency to follow certain well-defined patterns that have been set in every case by great originators. This does not mean that when a pattern is repeated, it necessarily becomes a weak copy of the original. The imagination that is found in good fantasy is an aptitude of the creative mind of the writer which takes a form that is personal to him. Each writer, though he may use the pattern of dream as both Lewis Carroll and George Macdonald have done, will express the dream differently because he has thought about it and imagined it differently.

There are other patterns than that of the dream found in the literature of fantasy. Perhaps the most significant among them are the quest, and the symbolic presentation of the natural world. Sometimes two or more patterns are intermingled; we follow a double or even a triple thread, and the pattern becomes more complicated.

Let us examine, for instance, W. H. Hudson's story *A Little Boy Lost*. The pattern the author follows is that of the quest, but are there not other patterns subtly interwoven with the main thread of the book? The story is about a little boy, Martin, who follows a mirage, and in trying to find it, becomes lost. We follow him as he explores the mysteries of plain, forest, and mountains until he reaches the sea and his wanderings are over. Martin's experiences along the way blend the mistiness of dreams and the realities of his expanding life. As Hudson tells it, the story is an allegory whose theme, in essence, is man's eternal search for the unattainable, for the beauty that stretches always just ahead of him but is never quite within reach.

Perhaps Hudson's underlying philosophy of life eludes the child who reads Martin's story. To him it will seem sad to be quite alone in the world as Martin is, even while he enters into his adventures with mounting inner excitement. But will not Martin's acceptance of the all-protecting power of nature waken in a child not only a sympathy with the wild things of the world but an all-embracing trust in life itself?

The power of nature to sustain and protect all who trust in her is Hudson's constant and recurring theme. He clothes it with the cool lush greenness of his imagery, he illuminates it with the intense light of nature where all is bright and still and waiting. The immensities of space and distance he envisions give room for the contemplation of universal truth. W. H. Hudson weaves native legend and myth into the story, and their indirect application to what he is trying to say enhances the truth behind the book's symbolic form. If Martin chases a mirage, so do we all, and Martin's story gives a sense of a universal experience and a universal urge toward the strange and beautiful in the world.

Coming now to the third pattern, Kenneth Grahame has given us a statement for all time of the symbolic presentation of the natural world. In a letter to Theodore Roosevelt, Kenneth Grahame describes *The*

Wind in the Willows as "an expression of the very simplest joys of life as lived by the simplest beings." He speaks of it again as "a book of . . . life, sunshine, running water, woodlands, dusty roads, winter firesides." In retrospect, the picture it calls up may be of Toad sitting on the dusty roadside in a kind of trance, uttering "Poop-poop!", a picture which recalls joy of new experiences told with the particular kind of rich, illuminating, and amusing—not merely funny—humor which the book contains. Or the picture may be of the field-mice singing carols outside Mole's "Dulce Domum" or of the "embracing light and warmth" of kindly Badger's home, bringing a sense of the obligations of friendship and the meaning of true hospitality. The most significant picture of all is that of the pageant of the river bank with the coming of the dawn and the music of the whispering reeds, as Mole and Rat work their way upstream, impelled to follow the sound of distant piping. This picture more than any other shows us Kenneth Grahame's view of the universe seen through the world of nature.

Few of us are awake to the beauty and wonder of the natural world around us. Kenneth Grahame has the winged words that lift us so that we see it with his sensitive awareness, and feel, too, the wider implications beyond what is visible. Mole, Rat, Toad, Badger and the others are not merely a mixture of animal and human attributes. They call up that deeper humanity that is universal, elemental, and revealing of our kinship with nature.

It is impossible to read *The Wind in the Willows* without a heightening of emotion and a sharpening of our perceptions as we enter into the excitement of Kenneth Grahame's feeling for the simplicity and beauty of nature—a world where instinct predominates. He sees the minds and memories of the animals as a race memory; as in the migration of the swallows to the south and in the odyssey of the seafaring rat as told in the chapter "Wayfarers All." The story is bound up with the familiar things of everyday life, but each contact with reality is made a springboard into an imaginative experience.

The Wind in the Willows is a rich book, the output of a rich mind. It is written with great clarity and lustre; its language is full of the incantation of verse. It is a joy to read aloud, for its rhythmic prose and for what Arnold Bennett calls "the woodland and sedgy lore in it."

Although the subject matter of a fantasy, like the pattern, may often be repeated in other books, it is not the subject matter nor the pattern which gives a book of fantasy the degree of quality it possesses. Its quality lies in the creative imagination of the writer and in his own personal expression of that imagination; in the consistent integration of his original idea with the drama of events; and in the integrity with which he gives verisimilitude and reality to the unreal world of fantasy.

There will always be people who do not enjoy fantasy. This in no way reflects on their literary taste, any more than the inability to like olives impairs one's enjoyment of other food. It does, however, restrict their pleasure in a field of reading which is singularly enriched by distinguished writing—a form of writing the enjoyment of which depends, more than others, on individual appreciation and personal taste.

Fantasy is timeless and placeless; it lives in the eternal country of the imagination and is never outmoded by succeeding social periods and conventions. In his introduction to *Reading I've Liked* Clifton Fadiman concludes:

> Twenty centuries from now . . . I do not see why people should not still be laughing and exclaiming over *Alice in Wonderland.* Among the few things resistant to the tooth of time, great fantasy is one, and great fantasy is always the special possession of children.[3]

ASSOCIATIVE READING

CHALMERS, PATRICK R. Kenneth Grahame. Dodd, 1935. Methuen, 1933.

DE LA MARE, WALTER. Hans Christian Andersen (in *Pleasures and Speculations*). Faber & Faber, 1940.

——. Lewis Carroll (in *The Eighteen-Eighties,* ed. by Walter de la Mare). Cambridge Univ. Pr., 1930.

MOORE, DORIS LANGLY. E. Nesbit. Ernest Benn, 1933.

---

[3] Clifton Fadiman, Introduction to *Reading I've Liked* (N.Y.: Simon & Schuster, 1941), p.xxii.

CHAPTER ELEVEN

The real justification of the novel as a way of dealing with the past, is that it brings home to readers the fact that there is such a thing as a world of the past to tell tales about—an arena of vivid and momentous life, in which men and women were flesh and blood, their sorrows and hopes and adventures real as ours, and their moment as precious as our moment. The power of the novel is that it can give to people the feeling for history, the consciousness that this world is an old world that can tell many stories of lost years, the sense that the present age is the last of a trail of centuries. It makes history a kind of extension of our personal experience, and not merely an addition to the sum of our knowledge.

H. Butterfield,
The Historical Novel

HISTORICAL FICTION

 To every reading boy or girl a book of fiction is first of all an adventure tale: "Is it a story? Tell it to me" is a universal response. If the living of an adventure story can be a joyful experience to a child, it is an experience which can be deepened and broadened by the knowledge that long before he was born the world was full of eventful happenings, stirring, marvellous, portentous; a world which he can enter through the pages of a story book.

In historical fiction there is first of all the story the writer is telling. Then there is the fabric of history into which the story must be woven as warp into web. The texture of the book will be fine, coarse, even, or patched according to the skill of the writer in weaving the two into one. The result is a fusion of imagination, chronicle, and writing skill. In its finest form, the historical story brings to a child, through imaginative response, an experience of living in other times. It brings a sense of the significance and color of the past in a way that transcends history. That is to say, the facts of history are always interwoven with intangibles, with human thoughts and feelings, and with the impact of the period on the obscure lives of whom history has no record.

The writer of historical fiction has first of all a story to tell, which should adhere to all the general rules of good fiction. But since it is also, in intention, *historical* fiction, it is a reconstruction of life in the past, an attempt to recapture the atmosphere or flavor of another time or age. If we are to measure the success of the writer we must first consider in what way historical fiction is unique as a form of fiction and what special considerations should be taken into account in judging it.

The idea behind the writing of a historical story is not to present the facts of history in readable form, but in going beyond historical data to give a way of looking at the past. Yet the closer the story stays to the significance of historical facts the more valid is the experience the author is able to give us through the world which he creates out of his own feeling for, and understanding of, an age different from our own. In reading historical fiction we are brought to see that though human nature does not change, human experience is different in each age and never exactly repeated. To catch the essence of that experience through the characters who live in the story, to savor the particular significance and feeling of a past age, is possible only when a historical story is written out of a mind steeped in the past. Only when an author has become sufficiently saturated with a period to move freely in it with a full awareness of the conditions and issues inherent in it, and sees his characters with sympathy and understanding as the products of those conditions, does a historical narrative of first quality emerge.

When Robert Louis Stevenson wrote *Kidnapped* he wrote a great adventure story that by common consent has a permanent place in literature. But since the world in which he sets forth the adventures of David Balfour is in the past, it is also a historical story. For this reason an analysis of *Kidnapped,* primarily a stirring narrative, should supply the clues to the discovery of those ingredients which make a good historical story. In that way we may discover also what to look for in appraising other historical narratives of a similar kind.

The theme of *Kidnapped* is Scotland itself, its moors and glens, its fog, and its rocky coast, all the characteristic and varied life that has shaped the temperament of the Scottish race. Because Stevenson's way of looking at Scotland is that of a writer who has steeped himself in its romantic history, it is only natural that his book should carry us back to an earlier period than his own, the period that followed the last defeat of the Jacobites.

The narrative relates the adventures of a famous Jacobite outlaw, Alan Breck Stewart, who is a kind of secret agent between the irreconcilable Highlanders at home and the émigrés abroad, forced into exile after the failure of the "cause." The plot is based on the celebrated Appin murder. The two chief characters, Alan Breck and David Balfour, are discovered near the scene of the crime and are pursued by the redcoats all the way from Mull to Edinburgh.

Skilfully Stevenson weaves into his plot the unhappy and impoverished state of the Highlands under the English oppressors. At the same time he makes it clear that it was not poverty and oppression alone which had broken the power of Scotland, but that clan feuds and rivalries played their part in dividing and disuniting the land.

In Alan Breck, Stevenson has drawn the personification of the Jacobite character. His bravado, his prickly pride, his fierce loyalty, and his ability to endure hardship for a cause he holds dear, all these highland traits are his. Yet he is much more than a type, he is himself— someone to know, someone we *can* know.

David Balfour on the other hand has the characteristics of the Lowland Scot; sound, rather prosaic, stubborn, yet fundamentally honest and true. "I am no blower and boaster like some I could name," he remarks when he finds himself inarticulate in comparison with Alan's eloquence. These Highland and Lowland traits are reflected in the subsidiary characters, the clansmen, the beggars, the preachers, and all the others who cross the path of Alan and David.

If ever the flavor of an age was caught, it is caught in *Kidnapped.* It is caught of course in the story itself, in its glimpse of the life at sea, the grimness of the slave trade, the insecure and adventurous lives lived in obscurity among the Scottish glens. But above all it is caught in the writing.

Considering the scope of the story, the telling is sparse and restrained. No unnecessary word or phrase delays the swift course of events or diminishes the drama. The strength of the writing is enhanced by the scrupulous selection of incident and detail; the dialogue is picturesque, using Scottish phrases of the period, which set the story in its age, with telling effect. Stevenson has a sure ear for inflection and there is a true Scottish rhythm and lilt to the speech of his characters; the speech of a race who easily burst into song or, like Alan, rejoice in a chance to take a turn at the "pipes."

Stevenson takes liberties with historical facts, but he defends himself for his rearrangement on the ground that "this is no furniture for the scholar's library" but is in intention an adventure story set in the past. At the same time he has so steeped himself in the records of the period that he goes on to say, "If you tried me on the point of Alan's guilt or innocence, I think I could defend the reading of the text." He knows his ground so well that he realizes (perhaps instinctively) where geography can be altered, or the passage of time compressed, and yet the truth, in all that matters to the period of which he writes, brings conviction to the reader.

Kidnapped reflects a mature mind, one that can simplify and clarify, and one that can resolve complicated politics and human relationships in an understandable and readable way. It is a story full of air and light and atmosphere in which his intention and his execution form a complete and realized unity.

If in *Kidnapped,* Stevenson has been successful in his attempt to reconstruct the life and to recapture the atmosphere of an age other than that of the writer, then to study his way of looking at the past provides some general principles to guide us in what to look for in the books of writers with an aim similar to Stevenson's. In other words it tells us what are the ingredients of a good historical story.

Another practiced writer of historical fiction, Sir Walter Scott, has given some helpful advice to those who attempt the writing of historical fiction. In brief, he believes that dignity should be preserved and grandiloquence avoided; that atmosphere should be attained without extreme use of archaic terms; that strength is necessary but that needless ruthlessness is to be deplored; that drama is essential but that melodrama should be avoided. He further states that there should be proportion without sacrifice of detail *and that accuracy of background must not crowd out human interest.* This last statement requires emphasis. It is so often the very thing which, in much tenuous and half-realized contemporary historical fiction for children, keeps a book from being alive.

These principles mentioned by Scott still hold, in the main, for books of historical fiction, and are worthy of attention. Although modern points of view have altered superficially, a reading of *Ivanhoe* or *Quentin Durward,* for example, convinces us that Scott has the root of the matter in his writing. As Saintsbury says, "we are indebted to him for the tradition of good form and clear style in English historical fiction."

In books of historical fiction for children there can be no question that *adventure* is the first requirement. The story must be concerned with action, and the closer the sequence of action, the more absorbing the story the book tells. Nor will children be completely satisfied if the action takes place only on the periphery of historical events. Story and history must be so joined and interwoven as to form inseparable parts of a single narrative.

The story itself is the foreground of the writer's picture of the past. As we have said, he follows the general principles of fiction in developing his plot and characters. But in choosing to set his story in the past, the writer also accepts the limitations which are imposed by the particular period chosen. Just what these limitations are has been clearly expressed by Helen Haines in *What's in a Novel:*

> It is true that in its nature the historical novel is fiction, not history: a work of imagination, not a record of fact. It seeks to recreate, not to transcribe; and the novelist is free to choose any subject that interests him and to write about it from any point of view that he wishes to take. But it is also true that his concern is with history in fiction and that he is under certain obligations to historic fact. He may . . . transpose time or reshape minor events to fit into his plot scheme; but he may not falsify history's fundamental record.[1]

It is their inspired working within such self-imposed and respected limitations that make Stevenson and Scott masters of the art of writing historical fiction.

The great difference between a good historical story and a poor one, apart from the writing, lies in the difference between a writer who is steeped in the life of a period and finds there a story to tell, and a writer who, with a preconceived idea of a story, looks for a suitably picturesque period for its setting. In other words, the difference is that though both writers are inventing fiction, the first is *in intention* a historical story while the second is any adventure story set in the past. The first claims to be true to the life of the past. The second may be a good adventure story but it is not a historical story merely because the characters are clothed in hauberks or in surcoats of silk. Historical fiction must be a fusion of story and period if it is to enrich and enlarge our picture of the past to the extent that it becomes a part of our experience.

Historical stories vary in type. For instance, the writer may invent the plot, the characters, and the incidents, or he may take the actual plot from history and utilize historical characters. Often he may combine both these methods, using for the purposes of his story both invented and historical characters and adhering in varying degrees to an actual historical plot. While it is true that writers of historical fiction often find incidents in historical record which suggest a plot, these incidents are usually not complete as stories. The source material has first to be absorbed, selected, and then translated into a living picture, through the craft of fiction.

In his introduction to *Men of Iron,* Howard Pyle mentions a plot

[1] Helen E. Haines, *What's in a Novel* (N.Y.: Columbia Univ. Pr., 1942), p.114-15.

against the life of Henry the Fourth which suggested to him the story of the book. He did not use the plot as he found it, but wrote a variation of it which allowed him to draw a living picture of the particular phase of the time which interested him. On the other hand John Masefield takes the outline for *Martin Hyde, the Duke's Messenger,* directly from history. The mad adventure of the Duke of Monmouth's disastrous attempt to wrest the crown of England from James the Second provides Masefield with his plot. In twelve-year-old Martin Hyde he invents a fictional character who is caught by force of circumstances in the fortunes of Monmouth. Through the boy's eyes we see the spirit of violence arising in the minds of men seeking power. We see the ranks of the common people torn on the one hand by the excitement of war, and on the other by the strong ties of domestic affection and duty. In vivid, forceful language, Masefield follows the rebellion to its defeat at Sedgemoor and the resulting "Bloody Assizes." The rebellion is made a symbol of all war: its waste, terror, corruption, and heartache, a picture which lingers in the mind of the reader. He also makes us feel a sense of the necessity of accepting defeat without bitterness, of meeting life with a good heart, with energy and ambition tempered by experience.

Incidents from historical sources are not only used directly as subject matter for an entire plot. They are also frequently fitted indirectly into the background, giving an opportunity to integrate the fictional characters into the historical events. For example in Conan Doyle's *Sir Nigel,* it is interesting to consider his use of Froissart's incident of the two knights, one French, one English, who appear before Poitiers with the same device on their hauberks. Conan Doyle gives the dialogue of this incident practically as recorded by Froissart, yet alters it enough to dramatize the story. In the same way he turns to account Froissart's description of the capture of King John after the battle. Without losing any of the pithiness of Froissart, by an ingenious twist he brings Nigel into the center of the picture and relates his invented plot to the historical setting. This is excellent handling of source material.

Writers of historical fiction are often faced with the choice between a literal presentation of the facts of history, thereby possibly losing the atmosphere of the period, and a rearrangement and selection of events which will give more effectiveness to the story. Historical incidents and events can sometimes be telescoped or rearranged without upsetting the balance of the picture of an age. It is another thing altogether to distort history for the ends of fiction. It is a confession of poverty of imagination and of a superficial, slipshod attitude toward the past, to choose, for instance, a well known event such as the death of a king and, contrary to record, bring it about by purely invented means. Such tampering with facts indicates not only a lack of the historical point of view, but a tendency to step outside the bounds of reality and thereby falsify the history of the period.

Reading the novels of Scott and Dumas we are aware of their historical approach to a story they wish to tell, an approach through records of the times of which they write. Through their assimilation of these sources of knowledge they are able to recreate imaginatively all the color and savor of another time than their own.

Let us see to what extent Conan Doyle displays the historical mind and the creative imagination as he shows them in his story of *Sir Nigel.* He has chosen the period of the Hundred Years' War, particularly the period between Crécy and Poitiers. From this period he chooses as his historical characters Edward the Third, the Black Prince, Chandos and, as well, the flower of chivalry of England and France. In addition he creates fictional characters, particularly his hero, Nigel, whom he invests with the chivalric ideals of the time. Nigel is the perfect knight "sans peur et sans reproche." To him he gives a task that would have been a joy to any of the knights of King Arthur's Round Table. Nigel fulfills his task with courage according to the highest tradition of the chivalric code. He does his three deeds for the honor of his lady and is rewarded on the field of battle by those words dear to heroes of his age. "Rise up" said the smiling prince, and he smote with his sword upon his shoulder. "England has lost a brave squire, and has gained a gallant Knight. Nay, linger not, I pray! Rise up, Sir Nigel."

Through the deeds of his hero, Conan Doyle fulfills what we have found to be the first qualification of a historical novelist. He tells a good story. He makes his characters live, but he does not lose sight of the fact that he is writing a historical story. So, carefully, but without obvious effort, he weaves his hero's life and adventures into the historical background of the time.

The period of which he is writing foreshadows the downfall of feudalism. The code of chivalry is still in vogue but something new is arising in the world. England and France are to emerge from the

170

Hundred Years' War as the two great nations of Western Europe. Chivalry is dying, nationalism is coming into being. This is the story that Conan Doyle is telling behind the story of Sir Nigel.

The new conception of nationalism can be seen in the person of Edward: "The tall stately man with the noble presence, the high forehead, the long handsome face, the dark brooding eyes." He is the soldier, the law-maker carving out a new and freer England, the personification of the new world which was being born. The barons were losing power before the might of kings. Nigel himself stands for the best of the old traditions, Edward for the best of the new thought.

This conflict behind the story that Conan Doyle tells is a powerful theme. Presented as fiction, strengthened and enriched by the added weight of history, the story makes clear the importance of the whole range of the issues of the period. All historical novels require such themes to give significance to the story they tell. Unless the writer evokes the forces which lie behind the historical events of the time, there is no true relation between the invented plot and the historical setting. Without this relationship a book has not the right to be judged a historical story.

Almost any period of history may be used as a subject for a historical story. Geoffrey Trease in *Tales out of School* says "there are no dull periods of history, there are only dull writers." But there are periods which, by the nature of their events or because of picturesque figures who walk through them, lend themselves more readily than others to historical fiction.

The Middle Ages is one of these colorful periods. Great issues of human freedom were at stake and new ideas imposed their accompanying events: the rise and fall of feudalism; the Crusades; the Hundred Years' War. For the writer's purpose, this period is fortunate in the contemporary source material available in literary form. Contemporary accounts such as Froissart and Malory provide that particular detail which gives exactitude and verisimilitude to a story. This, together with the wealth of books about this period especially written for children, make it a good field for examination.

While *The Talisman* and *Sir Nigel,* among other stories set in the Middle Ages, satisfy the strictest requirements of criticism, the books of such writers as Howard Pyle and Charlotte Yonge share the same qualities in a simpler way and to a lesser degree. These books have stood the test of time and are worth examining for the way in which they handle their chosen material and obtain their effects.

The Lances of Lynwood, by Charlotte Yonge, though simpler in conception has fundamentally the same theme as *Sir Nigel:* the foreshadowing of the downfall of feudalism, the emergence of the nation state. Chivalry was still the outward code but underneath was the surging life of a rising political power. The scene of the story, as in *Sir Nigel,* opens in England, crosses the Channel to France where the Black Prince, as governor of the important province of Acquitaine, holds his medieval court at Bordeaux. He was not, however, left in undisturbed possession and with the breach of the treaty of Brétagny, the Black Prince found himself cornered and short of supplies. He was free to take a stand and won a resounding victory at Poitiers. At this point *Sir Nigel* ends.

But the Black Prince continued his court at Bordeaux. His followers took part in sporadic skirmishes and he finally became embroiled in the affairs of Spain. It is here that Miss Yonge's hero, Eustace, joined his fortunes with those of his prince and accompanied him to Spain. The prince's friends and advisers were against a campaign fought in so poor a cause. This caused the estrangement between Chandos and the prince related in *The Lances of Lynwood.* The story deals briefly with the campaign, with the victory of the Navarettes and the prince's return to Bordeaux. It tells too of the prince's declining powers as his health fails, his loss of nearly all he has won. As the story ends he returns to die in England.

To the boy or girl reading *The Lances of Lynwood,* the Black Prince, John de Chandos, and Bertrand du Guesclin are probably not as important characters as the fictional hero Eustace. Yet his fortunes and adventures are so intertwined with theirs that the result is a living picture which underlines for children the fact that these historic characters actually lived as persons in their own times. Their actual appearances in the story, though brief, are lively, and leave a strong feeling for the essential character of each. This is shown in Miss Yonge's account of the taking of Du Guesclin prisoner by Eustace, and of Eustace being dubbed a knight on the field of battle:

> "You are the young Lynwood, if I remember right. Where is your brother?"
>
> "Alas! my lord, here he lies, sorely hurt," said Eustace, only anxious to be rid of prisoner and Prince, and to return to Reginald,

who by this time had, by the care of Gaston, been recalled to consciousness.

"Is it so? I grieve to hear it!" said Edward, with a face of deep concern, advancing to the wounded knight, bending over him, and taking his hand, "How fares it with you, my brave Reginald?"

"Poorly enough, my Lord," said the knight, faintly; "I would I could have taken King Henry—"

"Lament not for that," said the Prince, "but receive my thanks for the prize of scarcely less worth, which I owe to your arms."

"What mean you, my Lord? Not Sir Bertrand du Guesclin; I got nothing from him but my death-blow."

"How is this then?" said Edward; "it was from your young brother that I received him."

"Speak, Eustace!" said Sir Reginald, eagerly, and half raising himself; "Sir Bertrand your prisoner? Fairly and honourably? Is it possible?"

"Fairly and honourably, to that I testify," said Du Guesclin. "He knelt before you, and defended your pennon longer than I ever thought to see one of his years resist that curtalaxe of mine. The routier villains burst on us, and were closing upon me, when he turned back the weapon that was over my head, and summoned me to yield, which I did the more willingly that so gallant a youth should have such honour as may be acquired by my capture."

"He has it, noble Bertrand," said Edward. "Kneel down, young squire. Thy name is Eustace? In the name of God, St. Michael, and St. George, I dub thee knight. Be faithful, brave, and fortunate, as on this day. Arise, Sir Eustace Lynwood."

The writer, by such skilful and evocative pictures, sets the story in its period and links it to great events.

In *Men of Iron* Howard Pyle uses a different method. Through his reading and study he has absorbed medieval records and has made for himself a medieval world in his mind in which he is at home. He has not concerned himself so much with great events and great figures of history as with the ordinary experience of living in those times. This is the theme reflected in *Men of Iron:* a story almost without historical incident or characters which yet reveals a whole period through the experiences and adventures of its fictional characters. Howard Pyle gives an intimate picture of medieval boyhood through a vigorous and adventurous story whose events, never merely contrived, are implicit in the life of the age. We see clearly and understand the impulse that urged these medieval squires and knights to deeds of high personal courage.

Howard Pyle's background is always sound, his settings realistic and his stories entirely in keeping with the spirit of the age. He is less matter-of-fact than Charlotte Yonge. *Men of Iron* is a more romantic tale of "high and far-off" times than is *Lances of Lynwood,* for instance. It is a matter of individual choice which method is more effective.

An earlier, and younger, example of this difference in their way of "looking at the past" is found in comparing Howard Pyle's story of *Otto of the Silver Hand* with Charlotte Yonge's *The Little Duke. Otto* relies only slightly on historical events. Great historical figures are practically nonexistent in the story. The "Emperor," trying to control the robber barons of Hapsburg, is a vague figure in the background. Howard Pyle sets his story in the dark ages when the first dim light of "the new learning" is seen on the horizon of the European world, when the forces of the future are taking on an outline against the background of cruelty and destruction. This is the theme of *Otto of the Silver Hand.* Faithfully Pyle weaves his story into this great issue of the time. He pictures the subduing of the warring barons and the founding of the Hapsburg dynasty. He shows, also, how the better elements of the church cherished and preserved a love for the simple virtues and a love of learning at a time when nowhere else could they be found. All this he sets forth in simple (perhaps sometimes over-simplified) terms through the story of Otto, who is the symbol of the future. Unlike Miles Falworth, the adventurous hero of *Men of Iron* who wrests his feudal rights from his own and his father's enemy by force of arms, Otto's adventures are not of his own seeking, but are forced upon him by the cruel circumstances of the time in which he lives. Told in a simple, picturesque and, at times, poetic style, the book is an easily understood and memorable experience for the child who reads it.

On the other hand Charlotte Yonge's *The Little Duke* takes its plot directly from history, and historical events and characters form its background. When the story begins, the Norsemen have established themselves as powerful barons in the duchy of Normandy. At this early date they are still holding out against the forces which finally bring about the formation of the French nation. When the treacherous assassination of the Duke of Normandy places his small son, Richard, at the head of the Norse barons, their difficulties are increased by the necessity of defending the little duke's rights during his minority. It is true to fact that Richard when a child was taken as a hostage to the court of France; using the plot which historical records provide as a large sketch for her story, Charlotte Yonge fills in the human detail, the color of the age, and turns the whole incident into a picture and a story.

When considering any historical story written for children, whether about the Middle Ages or any age, it is important to keep in mind a measure—what a historical story can or should be. We can then see in what ways they live up to, and also how they fail to maintain the standard set up by the best historical fiction. It may be that a good story, competently told, will offset a sparse background as long as it does not betray its period. On the other hand a frequent cause for failure with young readers is the sacrifice of plot to period, with consequent loss of interest. The most common failure of all is the story in which the author contents himself with mere scene-painting; thinking by "prithees" and "I trows," by clothing characters in hauberks and chausses, by inserting historical incidents, to create a historical story. Nowhere in such books are the issues of the time, its peculiar problems, made clear. The author "works up" a period in order to set in it an unrelated story whose distance in time, he considers, lends it glamor.

One has only to compare such books with those of Scott, Conan Doyle, Stevenson and others of like quality to be aware of their defects. On the one hand there is the nice balance of history and fiction, the sense of period, the feeling for the issues that set the age apart; on the other hand a conventional story is projected against a shallowly conceived, picturesque background, described rather than brought to life, by a writer who has not understood the real significance of what he writes. The harm of such books is that the very mistiness and dim colors of the tapestry of history, in front of which the story runs its course, lend a sense of romance, of "far away and long ago," that disguises the emptiness of the content of the book.

The ultimate value of a historical story for children can be measured to some extent by the interest aroused in historical characters and events, and by the author's ability to give a unique feeling for a period. When we read about the Norman conquest or the Viking raids in Kipling's *Puck of Pook's Hill*, these far-off events take on color and vividness as if Kipling wrote from personal experience of the time. Such

175

imaginative reality, gained through complete familiarity with source material, characterizes the historical story of genuine worth. "It has a root in actuality and so makes us listen."

ASSOCIATIVE READING

BUTTERFIELD, HERBERT. The Historical Novel; an Essay. Cambridge Univ. Pr., 1924.

REPPLIER, AGNES. Old Wine and New (in *Varia*). Houghton, Mifflin, 1897.

SHEPPARD, ALFRED TRESIDDER. The Art and Practice of Historical Fiction. H. Toulmin, 1930.

CHAPTER TWELVE

I like books of knowledge; not those that want to encroach upon recreation, upon leisure, pretending to be able to teach anything without drudgery. There is no truth in that. There are things which cannot be learned without great pains; we must be resigned to it. I like books of knowledge when they are not just grammar or geometry poorly disguised; when they have tact and moderation; when, instead of pouring out so much material on a child's soul that it is crushed, they plant in it a seed that will develop from the inside. I like them when they do not deceive themselves about the quality of knowledge, and do not claim that knowledge can take the place of everything else. I like them especially when they distill from all the different kinds of knowledge the most difficult and the most necessary —that of the human heart.

Paul Hazard,
Books, Children and Men

BOOKS OF KNOWLEDGE

 A child is curious. As soon as he is old enough to observe the world about him he begins to ask questions. He wonders about all the external world that surrounds him, the change of day and night, of summer and winter, of opening flowers and falling leaves. The gift of wonder is precious and in its cultivation lies the best hope of a child's discovery of an unfailing spring of interest—an interest in the external universe which will not only train his powers of observation, but which will encourage him to explore and to find out for himself what he can about the world of which he is a part.

A child's growing sense of wonder includes not only the natural world which he can see and hear, touch, taste, and smell. He becomes aware of the human world of people. He observes patterns of human life around him, patterns of living which have evolved gradually from man's elemental needs for food, shelter, clothing, protection from enemies, communication, and transportation by land and water.

Our modern way of life holds complexity that is inexplicable to a child unless it is approached historically. Children are, at heart, Robinson Crusoes. They construct primitive shelters and dig caves even in city backyards where, for the time being, they discard our civilization and imagine they are beginning human existence afresh with only their own ingenuity to provide for their needs. In a child's interest in beginnings, in his wonder about the life and experience of early man in the morning of the world, he finds a perspective. As his knowledge increases he begins to see in proportion the world of today as it came from the past.

A child's instinct to learn comes from his wonderings, his curiosity. The more open his mind to wonder, the more sensitive he is to the satisfactions and enjoyments our earthly life affords. If he grows insensible to these because his natural, eager curiosity has nothing to feed upon, the result is boredom; a boredom caused by the lack of those resources of the mind which find never-failing interest in the wonder of the universe.

As soon as he can read, a child is attracted to books which give tangible form to the vague shape of his imaginings about his world. In this transition from wonder to knowledge and truth found in books can come a child's impulse to learn. Any mobility in the minds of children comes from the building up of those resources, inherent in their nature, of imagination, keen interest and the desire to know. Through association with universal experience, found first intangibly in books and reading, can come a child's earliest intimation of currents within himself that flow toward sympathy with the natural world and with human existence.

Children read what interests them. They read widely, indiscriminately, and uncritically everything that comes their way. The variety of their reading interests has been indicated in the foregoing chapters. But children, like adults, do not read solely those books of creative imagination in which they take such pleasure. They also read to find out, to *know*, about the bewildering, yet exciting world in which they find themselves. There is so much for children to learn that it is small wonder their eager, acquisitive, and curious minds seize on books of knowledge, books that will clarify and inform their minds to understand the things that are mysterious and unknown to them.

A child's willingness to accept and absorb knowledge from a book depends basically on the authority of the writer; on the thoroughness of the writer's understanding of the subject of his book. What is positive in his presentation will clarify and inform. On the other hand, a lack of authority will confuse and obscure a child's understanding, no matter how receptive his mind to learn what is unknown to him.

The object of writing a book of knowledge is to communicate to a reader certain information which the writer possesses. His skill can be observed in his manner of selecting and arranging the information he wishes to present so that it will convey the most enlightenment to the reader. In this primary aim of such books we can clearly see that the difference between a book of knowledge and a story book, for example, is in the *intention* of their authors. In the former, the writer has information to impart; in the latter, the author has a story to tell. In the telling of a story the author's whole mind and heart are necessarily engaged and his preoccupation is with the art of literature. This can only be a secondary consideration with the writer of an informational book. His interest must center in the special field of knowledge he is to present. If his book is for children he must take into consideration the uninformed and immature mind of a child. His concern will be with simplification of his subject with a specific age group in mind.

For this reason, informational books are infrequently literature and seldom do they survive the generation for which they were written. New ways of presenting knowledge to children are discovered in succeeding generations. Knowledge itself changes in the light of further discoveries and investigation. As a result of this process, informational books useful and satisfying to their own generation may be found inadequate and out-of-date for a later time. Whole classes of books of knowledge have been seen to disappear and to be replaced by other books which are more closely attuned to contemporary thought.

The transient nature of so many informational books constitutes one of the difficulties in forming a standard of judgment for books of knowledge, and is also the reason why this discussion is not centered around illustrative material. Except in the rare cases where high literary value is achieved in their writing, they cannot be judged by the standards we apply to creative writing, since the intention of the author of an informational book is different from that of the creative writer. What standards shall we then apply in judging whether a book of knowledge achieves its purpose or whether it does not?

The value, to a child, of informational books as a reading interest is not only in the present satisfaction of his desire for specific knowledge about a matter which has aroused his curiosity. A child may, for example, wish to construct a rabbit hutch and find in a book exact directions and diagrams which serve his purpose. His interest in rabbit hutches, however, is short-lived; and the knowledge of their construction, while temporarily useful to him, is unlikely to continue as a reading interest.

If his knowledge is to grow through the books a child reads because of his desire to know, it must be the kind of knowledge that grows with his growth. Even a simple, elementary presentation of a subject that has interest for quite young children can awaken curiosity and suggest extensions of knowledge through books beyond the one a child is immediately reading. His interest in the subject may thus become a reading interest developed through childhood into maturity. The

180

satisfactions of such continuous reading interests in the field of knowledge have permanent and rewarding values for children. Their reading of these books is complementary to their pleasure in creative literature, and both are necessary to the mental and imaginative growth of children.

What do children want to know? The answer is simple, yet comprehensive. They are curious about the natural world, and about human existence from the past to the present; from the people who live in the far corners of the earth to their next door neighbors. The extent of a child's curiosity may be judged from the breadth of content found in encyclopedic volumes which attempt to answer the questions a child may ask. Yet, like Kipling's Elephant's Child, there are few children who cannot think of "a fine, new question" that has never been asked before.

In general, there are three ways of writing books for children whose purpose is to inform. One writer may have information as his sole aim. Another, in giving information, also interprets the subject of his book. Still another (though this is rare) writes a book which not only informs and interprets but which is, in addition, literature.

In all books of information there are indispensable canons which their writers must observe if these books are to serve the purpose for which they are written. Accuracy of information, clarity of explanation, and acceptable use of the English language are essential and unchanging rules which must be regarded in all books of knowledge. In addition to these general canons, we will observe whether the information is scaled to the grasp of the reader for whom it is intended, whether the writer has the ability to arouse interest in his subject, and whether the diagrams or illustrations are explanatory and illuminating, if the nature of the subject requires them. These qualities are desirable in all informational books, but with differing emphasis, as we shall see when different kinds of knowledge are considered.

We have noted that the extent of a child's desire to know may be generally described as embracing an interest in the natural world and in human existence. Let us first consider the natural world. Under this heading could be listed what are called the "pure" sciences: astronomy, mathematics, palaeontology, geology, biology, zoology and so on. In considering books which deal with any aspect of pure science we find that there is an additional requirement to those already given. Pure sciences are based on theory, on scientific principles which transcend facts. These principles have not only to be stated; they require discussion, explanation and interpretation. In a book for children the subject of which is astronomy or evolution, for instance, complicated and abstract theories have to be simplified yet not distorted. Any simplification must still contain the essential truth of the principles involved. If these are beyond the grasp of children, as in the case of a subject such as mathematics, it would seem sensible to leave the subject alone as far as books for children's reading are concerned.

Knowledge of any of the pure sciences is never complete, so that the accuracy of the information given requires of the writer familiarity with the most recent scientific discoveries and with the works of accepted contemporary authorities. In writing books of science for children, the author should carefully avoid giving an impression that the last word has been said in any aspect of science. On the other hand a book of this kind should make clear to children that scientific knowledge is a process which, even in a specialized field, is incomplete. For example, here is a quotation from a children's book on the subject of astronomy which illustrates this point:

> One of the strangest supergiants is a star named Betelgeuse. At some times its diameter is only 180 million miles, which really is quite small for a supergiant. Then Betelgeuse begins to swell. It keeps on swelling until it reaches 260 million miles, and then begins to shrink. *No one knows why it does this, and no one knows whether it will ever stop.*[1]

This is a straight challenge to the scientifically curious child. It suggests to him that here is something to be pursued beyond childhood into maturity—that there are still worlds to conquer. The abstruse nature of much advanced science is beyond the comprehension of the lay mind. It follows then that such knowledge is far beyond the grasp of children. Science books for a child should make no pretense to definitive information, but as far as they go let us make certain that they are leading a child in the right direction. We can recognize that a book of science is trustworthy when it avoids the over-simplification which conceals the complexity and true nature of scientific investigation; when it confines itself to being truly introductory, thus suggesting the interest of further knowledge of the subject beyond the point at which the book leaves off; when it is written in a clear and lively

[1] C. L. and M. A. Fenton, *Worlds in the Sky* (N.Y.: John Day, 1950), p.78-79.

manner which make it understandable and enjoyable to the children for whom it is written.

Zoology, a far from winning name for the natural history of animals, has a peculiar interest for children. Their genuine sympathy with all kinds of animal life is recognized and the provision of books in this field overshadows that of any other scientific subject. Because of the diversified nature of this subject, different ways of handling and presenting the material have been evolved.

Many books of natural history for children retain the purely scientific approach although, keeping in mind the child for whom they are primarily intended, scientific terms are not necessarily used. These books should follow the rules for all good informational books for children. Many other books, especially those about the life and habits of animals, use the form of fiction to convey information. The use of this forms exacts the added requirement of satisfying the rules for good storytelling. Books in this last group may—and occasionally do—have literary quality as well as informational value.

Alert observation of animal life joined with sound knowledge of the facts should give a vivid, true, and unsentimentalized picture of whatever subject the writer selects if he has, in addition, a lively yet exact use of language in his writing. An animal story, if it is to inform the reader and interpret for him the world of nature about which he wonders, should excite his interest and curiosity as well as satisfy the desire of scientifically minded children to know the facts of animal existence, their reality and truth.

Turning from the books about the natural world to those books which deal with knowledge of human existence and human achievement, we find that we cannot entirely separate history from science. The history of early man grows more complete through the discoveries of archaeology and anthropology; the story of the early navigators and explorers is linked with astronomy and geography; the achievements of science have influenced the course of history. The modern historian even adopts the aims and methods of science in his investigation of the materials of history, whether they be written records or the results of archaeological research and discoveries.

G. M. Trevelyan has told us that history attempts to answer two great questions: what was the life of men and women in past ages? and secondly, how did the present state of things evolve out of the past? This is the most satisfactory definition I have been able to find of a subject of such a vast expanse of time and space, forming a backdrop for the phenomena of human life.

The province of historical knowledge is so extensive that in the brief years of childhood little more than an inkling can be gained of some part of what has happened in times past. It is all the more important, then, that whatever inkling a child may gain from his reading of books of history should be of a kind to whet his appetite for further knowledge. If the reading of history for pleasure and satisfaction is to grow with the growth of the child into maturity, we must discover what children, themselves, want to know about the past. We must consider a child's natural interests first of all.

We have seen that children are interested in beginnings; in the experience of living in early times and in primitive societies. Psychologists have told us that a child's development to maturity parallels that of the human race. Perhaps this explains the response of children's interest to such prehistoric societies as the mound dwellers and the cave men whose history is unwritten but whose life is revealed by the tools, weapons, and utensils they made and by the drawings they left on the walls of their caves.

A child has a natural interest, too, in what A. J. Toynbee calls "arrested civilizations . . . societies without a history." These are societies in which the rigors and exigencies of natural environment reduce life to the simple necessities of obtaining food, clothing, and shelter. The Eskimos and Lapps amid the Arctic ice, the Indians in the primeval forests of America, the Polynesians voyaging in their frail open canoes, the nomad Arabs in the Arabian deserts, the aboriginal tribes of the African jungles; these are some of the things in which children are naturally interested.

The interest a child takes in a book about the cave men, or the North American Indians, or the Eskimos, is primarily in their appeal to his imagination. As he reads, a child sees the life of a primitive people as a sequence of mental pictures into which, in imagination, he can enter and participate in the adventure of their precarious existence. He turns it into an imaginative game; a game that has realism for a child because the materials for playing it are readily at hand. With a child's aptitude for imaginative play, a vacant lot is transformed into an Arctic ice field, or into a Western plain, or into an African jungle. He absorbs the book's illustrations and diagrams of primitive dwellings and makes his own igloo in winter and his own wigwam or grass hut in summer. The tools and weapons pictured in the illustrations which are often reproduced from museum collections are re-invented by the child from whatever rough material he can find that can be made into a rough approximation of the original.

If a book about a primitive society is to have the power to conjure up in a child's mind a definite picture of an experience of life so remote from our own, the writer must meet an additional requirement to those of accuracy, clarity, and acceptable use of language. His ability to re-create the everyday life of a primitive society lies in whatever imaginative power he is able to bring to his knowledge of the subject. His success depends on whether he allows himself to be captured by his material, instead of superimposing upon it the stamp of a "dry-as-dust" recorder of lifeless facts.

To many modern historians, history is largely a matter of scientific investigation of disputed facts, a laborious effort to find out the truth about the past. A child's interest in history, on the other hand, comes first through the stories that history tells. To him, history is about men and the deeds they performed. He finds in these books about the past an extension of his reading of fairy tales and hero stories. Historical characters such as Leonidas, Jeanne d'Arc, Richard the Lionheart, the Black Prince, Marco Polo, and Columbus, to name a few of those who interest him in history books, are to him at least as real as Sinbad and King Arthur and Robin Hood. When a child discovers that the stories he reads in a history book are true, that these men and women actually lived and breathed in the days of yore, he is impressed with a sense of the continuity of life, of extensions beyond the living world he sees about him. His vague wonderings about the past take on reality and his imagination is stimulated by a sense of the color and fascination of those heroic characters who lived in times past.

Writers of history for children have recognized that a child's interest is in men and events, rather than in the growth of political and social institutions and ideas, and have often used a biographical approach to history. Children are perceptive of character in the historical figures of whom they read, and draw their own shrewd conclusions from how these people behave in circumstances which reveal individuality. The selection of the character-revealing episode or anecdote in telling the story of a historical person for children has value for a child because his mind is objective. Abstract conceptions of the truth in regard to historical characters and events can only be grasped by him when

185

presented in storytelling form. A child remembers it as a story, but it is also a story which relates the historical person with a child's understanding of his character as revealed by the story.

The early historians had an interest similar to a child's in their love of storytelling. They filled their histories whether of earlier or contemporary events with vivid description of happenings, and with anecdotes of the people about whom they wrote. The annals and chronicles of the early writers such as Herodotus, Froissart, and Hakluyt are among the most interesting sources for writers of history for children. The kind of material found in contemporary sources such as these arouse in children a curiosity about people in other times, in their deeds, in what they thought, and in how they lived. Through imagination turned on the past, children are able to picture and understand the experience of people in remote times and places. In this lies the great interest and value of history for children since for them it is the way the truth about the past is "realized, remembered and enjoyed."

Biography and history are often so blended in children's books that they are intermingled in children's minds as well. A child likes to identify himself with some character in a book he is reading, whether it is a character in fiction or one who actually lived. When a child knows that the people he reads about actually did exist, the fact that they once were alive adds immeasurably to the sense of pathos, excitement, and exaltation he feels in reading about Jeanne d'Arc, or Vasco da Gama, or Columbus, or Scott of the Antarctic. These stories, and hundreds like them, are clothed in the garments of fantasy: prison walls, kings and courts, unknown oceans, mountains of ice. They tell of hunger and feasts, triumph and defeat, life and death. The troubles and vicissitudes of their lives have for a child greater poignancy than he feels, for example, in reading the fairy tale about Rapunzel imprisoned in her tower. A child is aware that these are true stories of real people. They are not, like Rapunzel, the imaginary characters of the folk tale.

A biography, for children, is a story about a real person who has interest for them. If the book is to hold their interest, there must be a story worth telling about him that children would like to hear. The lives of all famous men and women do not necessarily have significance for children. A child's approach to biography is objective. He wants to know what the central figure of the book did, and how he did it. It is the *adventure* of his life that holds a child spellbound. It follows, then, that the lives of many of those whom adults call "great" seem unadventurous and uninteresting to children.

It is here that many biographies written for children fail to interest them. Their writers deal with people whose mature lives are beyond the child's imaginative understanding and whose early years are of slight interest. Not many people who become famous in mature years show in childhood their destiny of future greatness, and authentic records of their early years are seldom found. For this reason a life of the boyhood of Mozart, a child prodigy, can have more interest for children than that of, for example, Brahms or Shelley. The contemplative minds and lives of people of genius in the fields of literature, art, or music which give such pleasure to adults are seldom of interest to children whose delight is in action and adventure. Children have not enough experience in living to be able to view with sympathy and understanding the abstract ideas and theories which find expression in achievements in the arts by men of genius. An attempt to bring these lives within the understanding of a child will usually result in an over-simplification which leaves their greatness unexplained, because inexplicable, to a child.

The most natural and profitable protagonists of childhood, or adulthood, or both, as far as children are concerned are those about whom there is a story to tell; into whose lives is woven a colorful thread of adventure and romance. In the source material a writer uses, for a biography for children, he may find letters, diaries, and personal records which give a sense of intimacy, immediate experience, and added excitement to the story he is telling for children. To read the actual words of Jacques Cartier's journal which he kept on his three voyages to America, to read, too, of his observant interest in all he found in the new world—even the flowers and birds—gives a vivid reality to the whole adventure which a child is quick to feel. The log of Columbus' first voyage, brief as it is, holds breathless interest in its few pages which tell of the courage and faith that sustained the discoverers of the new world. There are as well the journals of Captain Cook (which ends so abruptly!) and of Scott of the Antarctic, among others which compel children's interest.

The lack of such firsthand authentic accounts, so revealing of personality, adds to the difficulty of the writer of a biography for children. Few people can tell the story of an individual both simply and revealingly. There is, for instance, the difficulty of explaining motives and actions without the psychological analysis of character which is outside a child's experience. To overcome this difficulty, writers often fill a biography with anecdotes and invented conversation which often make tedious reading and add nothing to a child's understanding of the person who is the subject of the book.

On the other hand, there are anecdotes which are related to the mainspring of the subject's life and ambition, and which reveal something about the man himself. Such well-selected and well-told anecdotes can give a child some insight into the mind and heart of the person whose story is told. The writer's authentic wide knowledge of his subject must precede that imaginative effort which brings vividly to life the person of whom he writes. The whole basis of a child's interest in biography is in its reality. To him it is a story, but it is also a true story. It must "come alive" and convince him of its truth.

The reading of history and biography gives perspective to any shortsighted attitude to life. When a child discovers that the life of his own time is only a point in man's long climb from his first appearance on the earth to his destiny in the unknown future, he becomes curious about life in other times and other places. He gains a sense of proportion, a balance that offsets ephemeral values and offers a point for reflection.

A child likes to put himself into the place of the characters of history and biography. The people he reads about do the things he would like to do. They live in caves, they fight bravely, and if not victorious they are heroic in defeat. They live in strange and marvellous places, they eat strange and unfamiliar food, their clothes and dwelling places evoke pictures of a world he has known in fairy tales. They live a life that stirs imagination and excites ambition and emulation. It is a kind of reading interest which gives extensions of experience; which arouses a child's sympathy with, and understanding of, the whole drama of human existence.

ASSOCIATIVE READING

Rowse, A. L. The Use of History. Hodder & Stoughton, 1946.

Stephens, H. Morse. History (in *Counsel upon the Reading of Books*). Houghton, Mifflin, 1900.

Trevelyan, George Macaulay. History and the Reader. Macmillan, 1946. National Book League, 1945.

ENVOY

Although children's literature may be dealt with under subjects as various as the chapter headings of this book suggest, let us not lose sight of the fact that each book stands by itself. It has its own value and its own relation to literature. We perceive this more clearly the closer a book approaches literature. When a child asks for "another book like *Alice in Wonderland*" or like *Treasure Island* or *Huckleberry Finn*, we are forced into a recognition of the singular quality that each of these books possesses, a quality unlike other books whose subject may be similar.

This uniqueness of quality is difficult to analyze because its influence is pervasive rather than apparent. The spirit of literature, when it is present in a book, is felt in the kind of response it arouses in the mind and heart of the reader, and though analysis can help us to a conviction that our feeling about the book has validity, we realize that it is implicit rather than defined. Yet the recognition of the book's quality—of the presence of the spirit of literature in its writing—would seem inevitable. The recognition that what we are reading is literature is seldom automatic. It is not so simple as that.

It is not difficult to learn to distinguish between bad writing and good writing. But in an age when competent writing is so general as to be almost taken for granted the problem becomes more complex. There are so many books for children that are correctly written in the facile vernacular of today; books whose skilful construction reveals the author's facility in the writing craft; whose themes reflect timely interests but which evade real issues, and which, on analysis, cannot stand up against straight thinking. There are so many books which present facts in glossy and attractive format but which in their content evade honest conclusions; so many books that are plainly time-fillers.

189

The unreluctant years

Children are not weary of the new and exciting world in which they find so much to interest them. They are not disillusioned "escapists" nor are they little "mass thinkers." They come to books as individuals, and ultimately it is still the simple values that move people, both children and adults, most deeply. The difference between the response of a child to one of these written-to-a-formula books in comparison with one which, like *Huckleberry Finn,* moves him to tears and laughter, vindicates our trust in the response of a child's mind and heart to what is fundamentally true and good.

Children read, through inexperience, whatever comes their way. In a time when children's books are almost a matter of mass production, it is possible that a child may pass from infancy to maturity without encountering one book that will satisfy him in his search for experience and pleasure; that will offer him reality in the place of a shadow of reality.

Children will defend themselves against encroaching mediocrity if the books of genuine quality are put within their reach. The miracle of the children's library is their "magic casement," their "open sesame," their "looking glass" through which they can push their way into whatever wonderland they will in their search for that inexhaustible country of the mind and imagination so full of wonder, beauty and delight.

A children's library which asks always of each book "is it *good* enough for children?", which has a sound philosophy of children's literature behind the choice and use of books, and which has worked out its own standards and values through knowledge, experience, and perception, such a children's library sustains and fosters the spirit of literature.

Every time a child reads of the heroic deeds of Beowulf, or goes with Mowgli on his night-wanderings in the jungle, or puts to sea with Columbus or Lief Erikson; each time a child floats down the Mississippi on Huck's raft, or follows Jason on his search for the Golden Fleece, the children's library is linking the child to children's literature, and so to all literature.

A child may not know that it is the spirit of literature that moves him when he takes these books to his heart, for his sense of criticism has not matured though his appreciation is high. But when he comes to the end and turns the last page of the book, he knows that, like *Billy Beg and His Bull,* he has "been undergoing great scenery."

INDEX